REACHING THE RIM

HOW BRITISH BASKETBALL PLAYERS CAN EARN COLLEGE BASKETBALL SCHOLARSHIPS IN THE UNITED STATES

BEN ALLISON

COTCH**HOUSE**
PUBLISHING

ISBN: 978 - 0615973388

First Edition

For my mother,

CLAIRE ELAINE JAMES,

who taught me that there's always light at the end of the tunnel.

I love you and owe you everything.

And my coaches, mentors, and father figures,

TONY AWCOCK

BILLY HUNGRECKER

who taught me that everybody is worth believing in.

CONTENTS

BEFORE WE BEGIN

Making a Full Ride a Reality

The Scholarship

Taking Action: What Can I do today?

Applying to College—the American Way

SCHOLARSHIP TIMELINE

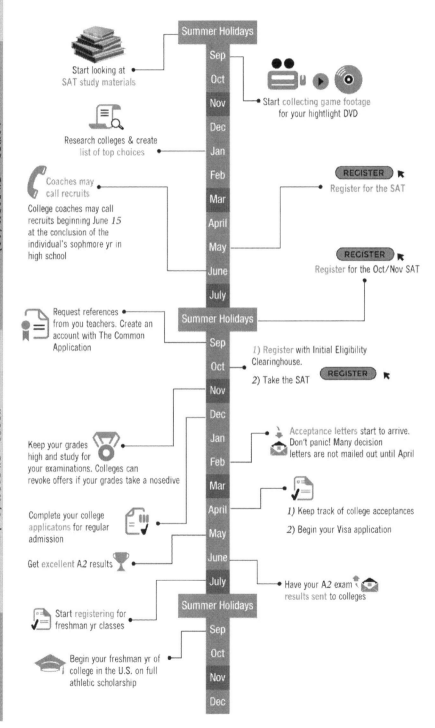

YEAR 11 — LOWER 6TH FORM (AS)

Summer Holidays

Start looking at SAT study materials

Start collecting game footage for your hightlight DVD

Research colleges & create list of top choices

Coaches may call recruits
College coaches may call recruits beginning June 15 at the conclusion of the individual's sophmore yr in high school

REGISTER
Register for the SAT

REGISTER
Register for the Oct/Nov SAT

UPPER 6TH FORM (A2)

Request references from you teachers. Create an account with The Common Application

Summer Holidays

1) Register with Initial Eligibility Clearinghouse.
2) Take the SAT   REGISTER

Keep your grades high and study for your examinations. Colleges can revoke offers if your grades take a nosedive

Acceptance letters start to arrive. Don't panic! Many decision letters are not mailed out until April

Complete your college applicatons for regular admission

1) Keep track of college acceptances
2) Begin your Visa application

Get excellent A2 results

Have your A2 exam results sent to colleges

FRESHMAN YR

Start registering for freshman yr classes

Summer Holidays

Begin your freshman yr of college in the U.S. on full athletic scholarship

BEFORE WE BEGIN

.

MY STORY AND WHY YOU NEED THIS BOOK

I've missed more than 9,000 shots in my career. I've lost almost 300 games. 26 times, I've been trusted to take the game winning shot and missed. I've failed over and over and over again in my life. And that is why I succeed.

—MICHAEL JORDAN

WINTER 2008, MADISON SQUARE GARDEN, NEW YORK

We walked into the arena and off the snow-covered streets of New York City though the back entrance of the building. Immediately we were funneled through a network of small passages lined with old paint, chipped pipes, and electrical cables that disappeared around the ever-curving passageway. It soon became clear that we were walking through the passage that circles the main arena. Back home on our practice court, in the college cafeteria, even in the classroom, my teammates were some of the loudest characters on our campus. They never stopped talking, cracking jokes or making fun of each other, but right before game time they were intensely quiet, signaling the calm before the storm. Like criminals chained at the ankles, we silently marched along the narrow hallway towards our dressing room.

As I looked around, the only things that broke the whiteness that covered the walls were framed photos of the

Garden's past performers, Elton John, Michael Jackson, Magic Johnson, Muhammad Ali, each face more impressive than the last. These framed faces weren't in a glass case nailed to the exterior wall of the arena or in the lobby for the Garden's ticketholders to see. It was more personal than that. They were displayed for those on the inside. Deep inside. These framed faces were meant for those who didn't require a ticket to the show. They watched us as we made our way to the stage. I felt as though they had recognized our presence and were giving us nods of acknowledgement as we walked by. A welcoming smile, perhaps even a line of salutes that seemed to say, "Congratulations son, you've made it".

Madison Square Garden is a truly magical place. If you ask any entertainer from around the world, be it an actor, singer or comic, "What is the greatest stage in the world?" the answer would be the same, "The Garden, of course". And it's no different for athletes. The Garden is home to the New York Knicks and reverently referred to by the rest of the world as the mecca of basketball. Every basketball player dreams of playing at the Garden, and what the old building lacks in traditional beauty it more than makes up in character and celebrity. I was a player on the Davidson College basketball team and we were about to take on West Virginia in the Jimmy V. Classic, a historic Holiday tournament held annually in New York. We had a talented team, ranked by the media as the 25th best college team in the country and our talents were about to be tested on the world's biggest stage. It was an honor and a privilege to be a part of the Garden's history and once we overcame the awe of this magnificent building we settled into our dressing room and got ready for the game.

Soon, the lights were on, cameras rolling, and the crowd of 20,000 had made its way off New York's 8th Avenue and found their seats. It was now only minutes before the game tip-off. I left the locker room and passed the famous faces one last time which spooked the butterflies in my stomach. I managed to calm my nerves and join the rest of my team at the entryway to the main floor. Our team captain took the lead. "Hands in", he ordered. We each raised an arm high into the huddle, fists together, and shouted in unison "1, 2, 3, WIN" before we ran out into the bright lights and gazing eyes, ready to do battle.

We won the game, and I had 10 points, including three dunks and seven rebounds in 20 minutes of play. This night will forever be one of my life's highlights. But I can assure you, my journey that led to this night was a lot less glamorous.

FAQ—DOUBTERS READ THIS

Do you have what it takes to become a Division I basketball player in the United States? Not Sure? Here are some of the most common doubts and fears among young players with dreams of playing college basketball.

Is it going to cost me a lot of money?

No. This book will show you the steps you'll need to take to increase your chances of being offered a full athletic scholarship. A basketball scholarship is an award of financial aid for a student to further his or her education while playing basketball. The goal is to save you thousands of pounds while playing the sport you love.

Should I already know people in the United States?

No. This guide will teach you to whom to reach out to and how to get their attention.

Is this how-to guide just for male basketball players?

No. Male and female basketball players go through the same college recruitment process. The governing body of college sports in the U.S. is very conscious of female inclusion and equality. Female student-athletes need be aware that federal law (Title IX of the Education Amendments of 1972, 20 USC 1681-1688) requires that athletic scholarships be distributed equally between women and men. Consequently there is a considerable amount of scholarship money available for women with athletic ability.

Do I have to be good at basketball?

Yes. This isn't a basketball training guide. It will not teach you training drills or provide tips for improving your game. This guide will help you put your existing skills in front of the right people in the hope that you'll get the opportunity to play alongside some of the most talented players in the world.

MY BASKETBALL JOURNEY

Birth   I was born in a town called St. Jozefziekenhuis in Belgium (or so it says in my passport; I tried to look the place up and it appears to have disappeared from the map). I have no blood ties with Belgium but my family had relocated for my dad's work.

Age 2   My family moved back to England and I arrived on British soil for the first time. We moved into what became our longtime family home in West Sussex. The West Sussex countryside is a great place to raise kids but not exactly a hub of basketball.

Age 8   The first basketball shot I remember taking was on a goal built by my dad in our back garden. It was made from a telegraph pole that had been pulled down and replaced in front of our house. My dad cut off a small length of wood from one end of the pole, dug a deep hole, and stuck it in the ground. He then leant the remaining wood against the pole in the ground so it jutted out over what would eventually become the court. He then fixed on a backboard and a ring, and violà! We had a basketball goal. We didn't have any concrete so we just played on the grass. Dribbling the basketball was tough and the hoop proved equally good for climbing as it did for playing ball.

Age 11   My parents went through a messy divorce and I was caught up in the whirlwind. Once the spinning stopped, I tried to refocus by dedicating myself to two things: academics (I wanted high grades) and basketball (I decided to put all other sports aside).

7

Age 13   I joined my first basketball club, Haywards Heath Eagles. My coach, Tony Awcock, became my mentor and would help me to develop my skills throughout my teens.

Age 14   I went to Dungarvan basketball camp in southern Ireland. I improved at a fast pace and this was my first time playing basketball abroad.

Age 16   I played basketball for an average Brighton Bears National League team. However, I did make the U16 England training squad. I used to catch the train from Brighton to Whitechapel in London for practice. Although an established practice player, I was never invited to compete in international competition. I was a skilled player, but physically I was a late bloomer and a little shorter than the other players in my position. I was told by the coach that I was "too short".

On the brighter side, I got a clean sweep of A's and A* in my GCSE examinations and earned a place at Christ's Hospital School (one of the most famous schools in England) for 6th form.

Age 17   I wasn't even playing for a basketball team at this point, just working out by myself with one goal in mind: becoming good enough to compete at the Division I level in the United States.

Age 18   I sent out to U.S. high school and college coaches hundreds of emails and more than 50 highlight DVDs. Despite a couple of positive responses, I received zero scholarship offers, so I accepted an offer to study economics at the University of York in England.

Age 19   I was playing EBL (English Basketball League) Division 4 basketball for Leeds Met Carnegie. It goes without saying that this wasn't the best league in England, or even second or third best. I'd all but given up hope of ever playing basketball in the United States. However, I made the most of my current situation by winning the regular season and National Shield titles. I was named the National Shield MVP and shortly after, I was invited to train with the Great Britain U21 team in preparation for a European Championship. I played well in training camp and was selected to compete for Great Britain in the 2007 U21 European Championship in Poland. Despite having arguably the most athletically-talented squad in the entire tournament, we lost critical games and placed 15th out of 18 teams.

Meanwhile, I was still writing emails and posting letters to basketball coaches in the U.S. I somehow managed to convince Davidson College basketball coach Bob McKillop to fly to York, England, for a day trip to see me play in person. After watching me scrimmage in a dusty university sports hall for just under an hour, he offered me a basketball scholarship worth over $160,000.

Age 20   I began playing for my new college team, the Davidson Wildcats. We went 20-0 in the Southern Conference before beating Gonzaga, Georgetown and Wisconsin to make it to the Elite Eight of the NCAA tournament. We were finally thrown off the road to the Final Four by the eventual champions, the University of Kansas Jayhawks. In the game, in front of 57,563 fans and millions watching around the world, our star player Stephen Curry, who became an NBA all-star with the Golden State Warriors, showed the moxie he's had all tournament, drilling an NBA-range 3-pointer with 54 seconds left that cut Kansas' lead to 59-57. Kansas went scoreless on their next possession and the ball was back in Curry's hands. Unable to get a good look at the basket as the clock ran down, Stephen dished to our point guard Jason Richards who launched a deep three. The ball was in mid-flight as the buzzer sounded. Then, the 25-footer from the top of the key thudded off the backboard. We were three points short of a place in the NCAA Final Four but our team ended up ranked 9th in the post-season national college basketball rankings.

Age 21   I played again for Great Britain in the U21 European Championships, Romania—this time co-captaining the team.

The same summer, I went on a European tour with Davidson College. We travelled to Italy, Slovenia and

Switzerland, playing pre-season games against pro teams in preparation for the upcoming season.

Age 23 After graduating from college, I played for Great Britain "Futures" in Germany as part of the Olympic development program. We went 2-1 in a series against the German Universities team.

My teenage and young adult life had been totally shaped by basketball and it was an amazing and unforgettable experience.

Before achieving success as a college basketball player, I went through the same rite of passage that every U.K. basketball player experiences: cold and dirty sports centers, bad officiating, countless hours crammed in the back of a muddy minibus, and the like. But once you come out the other side and finally earn your keep among the U.S. basketball elite, it makes it that much sweeter.

This guide will give you knowledge and skills to help you attain a basketball scholarship from a college in the United States of America. I have written this guide from my own personal experiences. When I was looking to get a U.S. college scholarship, I had no real instructions to follow. There was no path to follow and, to be honest, I didn't really know what I was doing. I had to work it out mostly by trial and error. Even now, there is no one correct way of getting a basketball scholarship. This is why, in creating this book, I have included information gathered from other English basketball players. Even though I have my own experiences to go by, no two players' journeys are the same. Every successful basketball player has traveled a different path and can tell a different story about how they reached success. And if you think you know the exact path you are going to take to become a college basketball player, you're wrong. You are in charge of your destiny but your journey will be unpredictable and adventurous.

LISTEN TO THE EXPERTS

When I arrived at Davidson College, North Carolina, in 2007 on a full-ride basketball scholarship, aside from myself, there were only 33 other U.K. basketball players playing college basketball in the United States. In the same year, the U.K. Department for Culture, Media and Sport conducted a survey asking children ages 11 to 15 which sports they had played, outside of school, in the past four weeks. Football was the overwhelming favorite, of course, with 47 percent saying they'd played it. Basketball finished at 15.5 percent, placing it behind swimming, cycling, walking and hiking and (wait for it), snooker! Even though basketball didn't prove as popular as some other sports, a surprising number of England's youth reported playing basketball on a regular basis. That's millions of kids. And from this population, only 33 of us had somehow made our way to elite U.S. college basketball programs. This makes us not only a rarity but also experts in the pathway of U.K. basketball players transitioning to the American game. After all, to be an expert in anything, all you need is a high degree of skill or knowledge, over and above that of the general population, and in a narrow field. I think we qualify. If you look again at the numbers I just mentioned, less than 0.1 percent of basketball players in the U.K. have done what I have done and it's my goal to open up this dream to others. So let's get stated by exploring the U.S. basketball landscape.[1]

1

Making a Full Ride a Reality

NOW IS THE TIME

Men talk of killing time, while time quietly kills them.
— DION BOUCICAULT

Time is a precious gift that we have all been given. Some of us use it well while others just sit idly by and watch it slip away. Some are scared to use it because they fear the consequences. But these people soon realize that sometimes languishing in the fear of failure is worse than fear itself. The clock is ticking. Now is the time. Seize each day. Use each moment. Be brave and follow your dreams.

The NCAA Men's basketball tournament, also known as The **Big Dance** or **March Madness**, is a single-elimination tournament featuring 68 of the best college teams. Although the NCAA tournament is only amateur sport, it has become one of the most famous annual sporting events in the United States. It's grown from an eight-team tournament to a multi-billion dollar sports phenomenon. In 2010, CBS, one of the largest U.S. commercial broadcasting television networks, paid nearly $11 billion for the television rights to the tournament. That's almost $771 million a year.[1] The tournament is the second most popular U.S. sports showcase for advertisers behind the National Football League (NFL) playoffs. During the 2011 tournament, advertising companies spent $738 million, with some television channels charging $100,000 for a 30-second ad during the opening round. The charges then escalated to $1 million per 30 second ad for the finals. Las Vegas casinos earn about $100 million each spring from bets on the Big Dance and in NCAA tournament bracket pools in workplaces and homes, Americans risk around $3 billion annually. That doesn't count the numerous contests put on by businesses that do not require an entry fee, but will pay out prizes to winners in hopes of getting people into their stores. The numbers become even more impressive when you remember that all this revenue is being generated just by the playoffs— we're not even counting the regular season revenue. It's safe to say that college basketball is a money-making machine. So where did it all begin?[2]

The Americans have created a tradition of winning in basketball since its invention in 1891 by Canadian-American Dr. James Naismith. Their global superiority in the sport can be seen from their record at the Olympic Games. America has been exhibiting its dominance in the summer Olympics consistently since 1939, winning 14 of 17 tournaments they participated in, including seven consecutive titles from 1936 to 1968.[i] While consistently impressing on the international stage, back in their home country, the Americans have created the most competitive basketball league in

---

[i] For those more astute readers who are questioning my math, remember, there were no Olympics in 1940 and 1944 because of WWII.

the world, the **National Basketball Association** (NBA). But before a player is touted as one of the world's greatest and joins the ranks of the NBA's elite, they must prove themselves worthy. Most players do this by competing in NCAA college basketball.

The inaugural college basketball game took place in 1901 when the University of Chicago, Columbia University, Dartmouth College, the University of Minnesota, the U.S. Naval Academy, the University of Colorado and Yale University began sponsoring men's games. Then, in 1906, the National Collegiate Athletic Association came to life, providing increased structure and organization to collegiate sports. But it wasn't until 1938 that the first national championship for NCAA teams, the **National Invitational Tournament (NIT)**, was organized. The NCAA tournament that people across the world know and love today would begin just one year later. Today, the NCAA is home to America's most talented amateur basketball players who showcase their exceptional skills in the most-watched basketball tournament on the planet.

At the end of each season, many of the brightest young stars must decide whether or not they should enter the NBA draft and forgo any remaining college eligibility. College basketball is a feeder pool of talent for the NBA. Each year, the NBA draft consists almost entirely of former college players, plus an increasing number of foreign players. While **club basketball** is the natural progression to the professional ranks in most European countries, college basketball is the pipeline for young players in the U.S. But with so many highly-talented U.S. players, the NBA, as you can imagine, is a highly-competitive league.

With only limited roster spots in the NBA, college seniors must face the harsh reality that their basketball careers are over. But as they keep alive their dream of playing professionally, some recent graduates have begun to look for playing contracts overseas. Europe has become a lucrative second option. There are a number of talented American basketball players dotted around the British Basketball League (**BBL**), but for most of them, England is just a temporary stopping ground to boost their stats and build their basketball resumes before moving on to bigger and better contracts in other European Leagues, such as Spain or Italy. Although these U.S. athletes aren't talented enough to play in the NBA, they usually become the franchise players in the BBL.

It's no secret that the standard of basketball in England is sub-par compared to the United States and many European countries. As British sport has monopolized rugby, cricket, and football in particular, basketball has often been left out of schools' sporting curriculums. As a result, few kids have developed lasting enthusiasm for the sport and therefore never got hooked enough on the game to develop into elite players. Few kids in the U.K. aspire to play in the BBL and so we're left with a lackluster professional league whose star players are foreigners. In comparison to professional players around the world, the BBL hosts mediocre players who draw in the neighborhood of 1,500 fans to each game. That's no Manchester Derby match but (and this is the good news), the popularity of basketball in the U.K. is on the rise.

10,000 HOURS OF PRACTICE

10,000 hours will do it. It was best-selling author Malcolm Gladwell who popularized the notion that 10,000 hours of practice was "the magic number of greatness," regardless of a person's natural aptitude. With enough practice, he claimed in his book *Outliers*, anyone could achieve a level of proficiency that would rival that of a professional. It was just a matter of putting in the time. Just clock a measly 10,000 hours on the basketball court and you'll be able to earn a living playing the sport you love. But wait a minute, let's do the math.

Most babies start taking their first steps between 11 and 15 months. Let's skip a few years yet still be generous and say that you start playing basketball at age 5. Now ask yourself: how many hours per week do you practice basketball. Three? Five? Let's again be generous and say you practice eight hours a week. At that rate, according to Gladwell, it will take you 1,250 weeks or 24 years to become a professional basketball player. That means you will be almost 30 before you begin earning income as a basketball player. But it's not your fault! Blame your country. In the U.K. it's hard to find teams to play for and places to practice. U.S. high school teams have organized practice at their school EVERY day. How are you meant to compete? Well, great players find a way.

Ten years ago, British players who couldn't find an organized indoor team to play for, or just couldn't find *enough* organized indoor basketball, started heading to the parks. With a lack of organized basketball in the late 1990s, **streetball** became a gateway into basketball for young Brits. Streetball can be hard to describe because its culture extends far beyond the basketball court.

According to Wikipedia, "**Streetball** or **street basketball** is a variation of the sport of basketball typically played on outdoor courts, featuring significantly less formal structure and enforcement of the game's rules. As such, its format is more conducive to allowing players to publicly showcase their own individual skills."

The growth of streetball was catalyzed by a clothing brand called AND1. This company separated itself from the Nike and Adidas empires with a marketing slogan that was a clarion call for an anti-establishment basketball revolution: *Get Yours.*

At first, shoes and t-shirts were AND1's bread and butter. The company had a line of illustrated "trash talk" t-shirts with lines like "Give 'N' Go. Give up the Game and Go Home!" written across the chest. Its stylish and fresh shoes came with a free VHS AND1 mixtape. There was a lack of televised basketball on terrestrial TV and I remember being more excited about getting home and watching the VHS to see pro streetballers Hot Sauce and Robert Martin (AKA 50) in action than I was wearing the shoes for the first time. These videos showcased a style of basketball that had attitude. AND1 flung the middle finger in the face of tradition; it was the hip-hop generation colliding with old-time values on the basketball battleground. AND1 turned the old school of basketball into a new school of showmanship where the biggest stars and brightest reps were manufacturing style over substance, humiliation over humility.

Every weekend I remember taking an hour-long bus ride to Brighton, my closest city, to play on the beach court and check out the latest AND1 gear in the Foot Locker inside the nearby shopping center. I used to do this with the regularity of a priest visiting church on a Sunday. Basketball was my religion and streetball my denomination.

Shortly after AND1 hit the U.K. basketball scene, the Web site *streetball.co.uk* was launched, providing a source of localized basketball news for British ballers. And with no competition in the market, *streetball.co.uk* became the cornerstone of U.K. basketball culture. Whether you were an actual streetballer, played on an organized indoor team or were just a basketball enthusiast, *streetball.co.uk* was the place to go to watch videos, check out the latest apparel and get information on basketball events around the country. *Streetball.co.uk* achieved a cult following in the U.K. As basketball grew in popularity and became more organized, *hoopsfix.com* emerged on the scene, launching in 2010.

Hoopsfix.com covers U.K. ballers playing ball in Europe and the U.S., as well as all Great Britain men's and women's teams. It's a testament to how British basketball has grown. Now that the profile and popularity of basketball is increasing as a country, Britons must be able to support its growth.

THE U.K. BASKETBALL LANDSCAPE

In order to build on the momentum and carry us into to the new era of British Basketball, government funding must grow in line with basketball's increasing popularity. Currently, basketball is underfunded by Sport England, the governing body responsible for distributing funds. In January 2013 the agency said the sport had not done enough to prove it could win a medal at the 2016 or 2020 Olympics and would lose its £8.5m backing for the next Olympic Cycle. If this decision had stood, Great Britain would have had no hope of entering a team in the 2016 Olympics in Rio de Janeiro.

However, the basketball community did not take this decision lying down. NBA and Chicago Bulls forward Luol Deng promptly sent a letter to Prime Minister David Cameron expressing his discontent and confusion over the announcement. Deng, like many others in the U.K. basketball community, believes that basketball in Great Britain has come a long way in the past few years. And the Great Britain national team is one of the main reasons British basketball is being pulled into the spotlight. For example, in 2011, after a 28-year absence from any major basketball event, the Great Britain national team showed itself as a revived force in international competition after outdoing all expectation during the Eurobasket 2011[ii]. Again in 2012, the Great Britain Olympic team proved itself as an international competitor, beating China and narrowly losing to the eventual finalist, Spain.

Along with Great Britain's encouraging performance on the court, there has been a lot of basketball buzz off the court as well. During the past few years, London has been the host city for several NBA regular-season games. Each time, the teams have been welcomed by sellout crowds and overwhelming media attention. ESPN American now channels NBA and U.S. collegiate basketball

---

[ii] EuroBasket is the main basketball competition contested biennially by the men's national teams governed by FIBA Europe

to television screens in European homes. You cannot argue the fact that the standard and profile of European basketball, the United Kingdom included, is on the rise. "It's incredible how far this team has come," says Deng. Deng believes that the London 2012 Olympics were meant to be the start of a "legacy" brought to all sports in the U.K., including basketball. The funding cut would demolish the legacy the GB senior men's team has worked so hard to build. Momentum would be lost, interest would be lost. We would again have nothing to bestow to future generations of young players. "How are we supposed to motivate these kids to carry along their journey when there's now nothing at the end?" says Deng. "No Team GB, no Olympic dream, no goal." And he's right.[3]

Because of a very vocal public campaign, Deng's letter, and a number of impressive presentations to the U.K. sport board, the funding reprieve was overturned. Great Britain basketball wasn't awarded the same $8.5m they had received for the London Olympics but it it was promised one year's funding, with the rest conditioned on the fulfillment of "strict performance criteria." This was a huge day for British basketball. It showed how much people in the U.K. cared about basketball, and how much buzz there was among new enthusiasts and people on the sports periphery.

With the Great Britain team back in action, our nation's goal is back in sight, not just for the senior players but for everyone involved in British basketball. The hard part of lighting the fire is getting it started; but once it takes hold, there's no stopping it.

If you still aren't convinced by any of this, listen to this: before 2012, the last time Great Britain qualified for the Olympics was 1948. Britain went 0-5 and was outscored 298-103.[4]

Hey, we're making progress. But how does all this impact your chance of playing basketball in the U.S.?

THE FOREIGN RECRUITING NETWORK

Over the five year period from 2008-2013, 3,428 foreigners played pro or college basketball in the United States, and only 127 of them were from the United Kingdom.[5] During the 2007-08 season (my freshman year in college), there were only 33 players from the U.K. competing in U.S. college ball. In 2013 it was almost double that number. In short, the foreign recruiting network is small but rapidly expanding as coaches are looking more and more for overseas talent.[6] Here are a few of the main reasons why:

Reason 1. There's greater competition among Division I programs for a talent-pool that's being tapped by an increasing number of colleges playing championship-caliber basketball in Division I. In other words, American high school recruits now have a larger number of competitive programs to choose from. Look at some of the mid-major teams that have made deep runs in the NCAA tournament during the last few years. George Mason led the way in 2006, making an unexpected Final Four appearance. Mid-major Davidson made a fairytale run to the Elite Eight in 2008, followed by the unforetold winning streak of the Butler Bulldogs as they battled their way to back-to-back National Championship games in

2010 and 2011. Five to ten years ago, success of mid-major teams in the post-season was unheard of. But now, it's not only expected but keenly anticipated, as everyone loves to see a good upset. In the 2013 Big Dance, mid-major Gonzaga was awarded a deserving #1 seed after it dominated the regular season, finishing 32-3.

What does all this tell us? We can no longer use the "David and Goliath" fable to describe games between major and mid-major teams because in today's collegiate basketball, there really is no underdog. So: say I'm a top high school recruit trying to decide on a college. Do I choose Duke with its history of winning and long list of alumni who have gone on to play in the NBA? Or do I choose Gonzaga, a mid-major on the rise with recent success and media buzz? It used to be an easy choice. But now, the top schools are losing their recruits to the mid-majors.

Reason 2. The population of talented U.S. college players is actually shrinking—a problem accentuated by the "**One and Doners**." "One and Done" is a slang term used to describe a player who stays in college for one year before bolting for the NBA. The phrase was popularized in 2005 after the NBA and its players added an age limit that required players entering the draft to be 19 years old or to have completed their freshman year of college (For a number of reasons, the NBA didn't want so many of its players to come straight out of high school). As a result, players would complete their freshman year (probably not even going to class their second semester after maintaining a barely-sufficient GPA to play after their first semester) and then jump ship. Gone are the day's great players such as Grant Hill, Steve Nash or Tim Duncan who stayed in college all four years. [7]

Reason 3. Tighter academic standards are deterring many good players from attending the college they were hoping to play ball for. In 2012 the NCAA made some drastic academic changes that were put into effect for the graduating class of 2016. The minimum GPA for the 16 required core courses was bumped up from a 2.0 to a 2.3, while 10 of those 16 core courses are now required to be completed by the end of the athlete's junior year. It doesn't sound like much — banging out a C+ average instead of a C shouldn't really be all that difficult — but these are significant changes as many college athletes gain initial eligibility by the skin of their teeth or load up on core courses in their senior year to make up for spending their first three years as goof-offs. The NCAA estimated that 43 percent of men's basketball players who entered college in 2009 would have been acedemically ineligible in 2016.[8] Let's assume that number is accurate for every incoming class, and two starters on every team in the country would not have been eligible as freshmen. That's a huge number. Future college players who are teetering on the edge of academic ineligibility must do their due diligence and knuckle down in the classroom in order to play college ball. But at the end of the day, stricter academic requirements mean that more and more U.S. players just aren't going to make the cut.

Reason 4. Players who can make an immediate impact, particularly at the center position, are scarce. Let's take a moment to consider

Dwight Howard[iii]. Howard is one of the finest players in the NBA but, in my humble opinion, a basketball talent operating way below his potential. He wears the flashy gear and excites the crowd with tremendous dunks but lacks all the fundamental skills that European big men use to make a living. Effective post players are so scarce that the Miami Heat won the 2013 NBA championship without a true center. Think about how good they *could* have been.

Now add the fact that through media channels and improvements in transportation, foreign players have become more accessible. It can be slim pickings at times for college recruiters. And when college recruiters can't find talent at home, they will start looking overseas. The opportunity for foreign basketball players to play college basketball in the United States has never been better.

Here are a few additional thoughts: A coach can recruit you (a foreign player) after you make initial contact, without much fear of your being well-known in recruiting circles and therefore having to compete against other colleges for your services. When you contact coaches from outside the U.S., they are usually eager to find out who you are, and hope that you'll turn out to be a hidden treasure for them. A couple of negatives are that the coaches will have to evaluate the talent you play against, and your recruitment will require more logistics than those of a U.S. player. No college coach is going to offer you a scholarship without seeing you play in person, somewhere in the world. Again, this can be overcome by

---

[iii] Dwight Howard is an 6'11'' American professional basketball player for the Houston Rockets of the National Basketball Association (NBA).

initiating your recruiting contacts early and being aggressive when contacting schools. Remember: seize the day, be confident, and follow your dreams.

"THE 33"

We'll call them "The 33" — the 33 British players playing in college during my freshman year, 2007-2008. But why them? Why did so few make it? "The 33" can be separated from the millions of other young people playing basketball in the U.S. based on their goals and their unstoppable determination. Below is a quote from Steve Jobs, entrepreneur, marketer, and inventor, who was the co-founder, chairman, and CEO of Apple, Inc. The quote pinpoints the similarity between "The 33" and the difference between them, and those who don't quite make it to U.S. college stardom:

As you grow up, you're told the world "is the way it is" and your life is just to live your life inside the world and try not to bash into the walls too much; try to have a nice family life; have fun; save a little money. But that's a very limited life. Life can be much broader once you discover one simple fact: Everything around you that you called "life" was made up by people who were no smarter than you. And you can change it. You can influence it. You can build your own things that other people can use. And the minute you understand that, you can poke life…. As soon as you push in, something will pop out the other side, that you can change it, you can mold it…. That's maybe the most important thing. Shake off that erroneous notion that life is just there, and you're just going to live in it. Once you learn that, you'll never be the same again.

-Steve Jobs, 1995

The realization Steve Jobs is talking about is the thing that makes "The 33" different: the willingness and courage to break out of the mold and go after something they're passionate about. This is the key distinction. You merely need to realize that it's possible for you, and then build the confidence to go after it.

How to Build Self-Confidence

Below is an email sent from Davidson College head coach Bob McKillop to his players on November 29, 2007, midway through that special season that ended with a 20-0 Southern Conference record and a run to the NCAA Elite Eight. In his email, McKillop talks about confidence, something every living person struggles with at one time or another.

From: Bob McKillop
To: Team
Date: 11/29/2007, 11.36 AM

Fellas,

We have so many gifts. We are athletic. We are skilled and talented. We are winners from our experience of winning. We are smart and learners and we get better. We are workers and continue to commit ourselves. All of these are talents and if we blend them together with a trusting attitude and the unselfish spirit that seems to be part of our locker room and our team fabric, anything can happen for us. But, we must use all of these wonderful gifts and talents that we have.

We all must confront our feelings and our fears. I'm no different than you. I'm sometimes tempted to have some doubts, to not be as confident as I should be. But, I have disciplined myself to refuse to give in. I dwell on the three words of Caring, Committing, and Trusting. I constantly repeat to myself the three objectives that we have: Let's get better. Let's have fun. Let's play to win. However, as much as I discipline myself, the temptations are always hovering. I run. I daydream in the car. But the temptation is always there. And then, one of our coaches says something positive, or a former player calls and reminds me of how special and proud he feels to be part of our tradition, or one of you reminds me about our Code and what our objectives are. And then I figure it out. We have become an incredible army, an incredible family. That's the greatness and strength of who we are. It doesn't mean that we're all lovey-dovey but it does mean that we hold each other accountable and reinforce each other.

I used to fear that people would write or say that I was not a good coach or smart coach. I no longer have that fear because I know how hard I will work to help us. I know how much I care about you. And I know how confident I am in your talents and our preparation. I've truly come to understand how much I need all of you and that I am nothing as a coach without you.

Confidence is a choice. It's defined as being certain, having trust. You choose that. You decide that. With you on my side, with us on each other's side, that should be an easy choice for us. Let's get better. Let's have fun. Let's play to win.

Coach

So let's go out and grab it. But first, we must know what we are shooting for. We can do this by answering the question: What is an athletic scholarship?

2

The Scholarship

HOW DO SCHOLARSHIPS WORK?

"These are my new shoes. They're good shoes. They won't make you rich like me, they won't make you rebound like me, they definitely won't make you handsome like me. They'll only make you have shoes like me. That's it."

—CHARLES BARKLEY

College education in the United States can be very expensive. It's typically more expensive than university in the United Kingdom and affording college tuition can be a daunting prospect for most students. As of October 2010, according to CNNMoney.com, without financial aid the average annual cost of a public university is $7,605. This is around £5,000. Private universities, on the other hand, are substantially more expensive than public. At private four-year institutions, the average annual cost was $27,293 as of October 2010. This is £18,000. For most Americans, there are ways to make college more affordable, but financial loans for international students are hard to come by. Americans have the option of getting a financial reprieve by studying at a public school in their home state. For example, students living in North Carolina who study at The University of

North Carolina don't have to pay as much as out-of-state students. International students obviously do not qualify.[1] But you're in luck, although you may not know it, you have created a workaround for this financial roadblock. By working hard on the basketball court, you may have made yourself eligible for, essentially, free money for a college education. You just need to know how to get your hands on it.

A **scholarship** is a form of financial aid for a student to further his or her education. Scholarships are designed to reduce the financial burden and are awarded based on various criteria such as merit or need. Scholarship money is not required to be repaid. An **athletic scholarship** is a form of scholarship to attend a college or university which is contingent on the applicant's athletic abilities. This is why athletic scholarships are decided by the athletic coaching staff. If a coach thinks that you will add value to their program, they will extend an offer of financial aid for you to join the team and study at their university. A **"full ride"** basketball scholarship will pay for your tuition, room, board, and books, generally for the entire time you are enrolled at the college/university. That's the basic principle, but in reality, the recruitment process, with respect to earning a scholarship, is a lot lengthier and more complicated than this.

WHO OFFERS BASKETBALL SCHOLARSHIPS?

College basketball scholarships are offered at the NCAA **Division I**, NCAA **Division II**, **NJCAA** and **NAIA** levels.

The Scholarship

Division I

Generally, the most talented players play in NCAA Division I and this is where the most scholarship money lies. Each NCAA Division I school can offer 13 full scholarships. Within Division I you also have different levels of competition based on your conference. Some conferences are considered more competitive that others and have better teams that attract more talented players. These conferences are known as **major conferences**. There are six major conferences: the Atlantic Coast Conference (ACC), Southeastern Conference (SEC), Big East, Big 10, Big 12 and Pac-12. **Mid-major** is a term used to refer to athletic conferences that are not among the major six but are still highly competitive. It's believed that the term "mid-major" was coined by the sports media to distinguish the Bowl Championship Series (BCS), the power conferences in collegiate American Football, from non-BCS conferences. Now, mid-major is used casually to describe middle-of-the-road Division I teams. But because the term is not officially used by the collegiate governing body, you don't really need to dwell on it. There are a few things, however, that you should know.

Basketball is considered a **head count sport** for both men and women in NCAA Division I. This means that all scholarships offered are full scholarships. In all other divisions, basketball is considered an **equivalency sport**, which means that coaches can divide the value of the total scholarships allotted among as many players as they like. Scholarship money that has been divided up and offered to a student to cover only part of his or her tuition and/or boarding is called a **partial scholarship**. Coaches will use the ability to distribute scholarship money among players to their advantage. Even a small offer of financial aid to a college recruit can be a big incentive when deciding between schools. So, as a strategy, coaches will tend to offer more financial aid to desirable recruits than they would less desirable recruits. But if you are a true Division I-caliber player, you won't have to worry about this, as all Division I scholarships will cover the full cost of tuition, room, board and books.

Examples of high-major Division I schools include: the University of Michigan; the University of Tennessee; the University of Notre Dame; and Vanderbilt University. Examples of mid-major Division I schools are: Middle Tennessee State University; the University of Tennessee-Chattanooga; and Kent State University. Examples of low-major Division I schools are: Tennessee State University; Gardner-Webb University; and Kennesaw State University.[2]

Division II

Division II schools cannot offer as many basketball scholarships as Division I schools. NCAA Division II basketball limits its member institutions to a maximum of 10 full scholarships. Just like Division I, a full scholarship consists of tuition, room, board, and books. Many Division II student-athletes pay for school through a combination of scholarship money, grants, student loans and employment earnings. Division II athletics programs are financed within the institution's budget just like other academic departments on campus, so there are maximum financial aid awards for each sport that a Division II school must not exceed. Division II teams usually feature a number of local or in-state student-athletes and traditional rivalries with regional institutions dominate schedules of many Division II athletics programs.

Division II schools consist of smaller public universities and many private institutions, and a good number of scholarships go to student-athletes who transfer from Division I schools. A transfer student does not have to sit out a year before resuming sports participation as would be the case in the event of transferring from one Division I institution to another (we will discuss this later in more detail).

The highest-ranking NCAA II teams are often of a higher caliber than the lowest-ranking teams of Division I, so it's safe to say that there's a lot of talent in Division II as well. Some players face a tough decision when deciding between DI and DII colleges. If they choose Division II, they could possibly become a star; on the other hand, if they choose a Division I school they may become a "small fish in a big pond" and spend four years riding the bench.

Examples of NCAA Division II schools are: Carson-Newman University; Tusculum College; Clayton State University; and Lincoln Memorial University.[3]

Division III

Unlike Divisions I and II, NCAA Division III does not offer athletic scholarships but does offer other forms of financial aid, usually academic scholarships. Division III athletics features student-athletes who receive no financial aid related to their athletic ability, and athletic departments are staffed and funded like any other department in the university. Division III athletics departments place special importance on the impact of athletics on the participants rather than on the spectators. In that sense, it's less commercial and business-like than Division I. The student-athlete's experience is of paramount concern, and hence Division III athletics encourages participation by maximizing the number and variety of athletics opportunities available to students. In Divison III, primary emphasis is placed on regional in-season and conference competition.

As Division III schools do not offer athletic scholarships, recruiting tactics are limited and the level of play varies greatly from team to team. Examples of NCAA Division III schools are: Maryville College; Covenant College; Sewanee: The University of the South; Rhodes College; Huntingdon College; Birmingham Southern College and Oglethorpe University.[4]

NJCAA

The **National Junior College Athletics Association (NJCAA)** is made up of "two-year schools" and is also divided into three divisions. NJCAA Division I schools can grant athletes a full athletic scholarship. Division II schools can offer only partial scholarships that cover tuition, books and fees, while Division III colleges cannot offer any.[5] Take a look at the following table, showing the number of participating schools and scholarships available in men's and women's college basketball.

Men's Basketball	Participating Colleges	Scholarships	Women's Basketball	Participating Colleges	Scholarships
NCAA DI	344	13	NCAA DI	342	13
NCAA DII	282	10	NCAA DII	281	9
NCAA DIII*	403	0	NCAA DIII*	426	0
NAIA	255	17	NAIA	256	12
NJCAA	560	15	NJCAA	519	24
Total	**1,844**		**Total**		**1,824**

*NCAA DIII schools do not offer athletic scholarships but do offer other forms for financial aid. [6]

Now that you've seen the numbers above, consider for a moment the number of basketball players in the U.S. who are high school seniors that share the dream of playing basketball in college. Now add the thousands of international players with the same goal. What you have is life's most fundamental dilemma: infinite wants and limited resources. You have hundreds of thousands, maybe millions, of people your age across the world who dream of playing American college basketball, but fewer than 5,000 available college roster spots per year. The numbers just don't add up. So the question you need to concern yourself with is: How will I separate myself from the competition?

DARE TO DREAM "BIG"—-REALISTICALLY

The English poet Robert Browning once said: "Ah, but a man's reach should exceed his grasp – or what's a heaven for?" He's saying that to achieve anything worthwhile, a man should attempt those things that may turn out to be impossible. This should be the shared quality of all great men. But at the same time it also suggests that people tend to end up unhappy because they always want what they can't have. With this in mind, it's important that you strive for greatness by setting a series of realistic goals. It's a balancing act; you want to strive to be the best but you don't want to take too big of a leap and fall short. For instance, if you are a Division III-level athlete who only applies to Division I schools, you're setting yourself up for failure. You need to think strategically regarding the number of DI, DII, and DIII schools you apply to.

ANSWERING THE "WHATS" OF U.S. EDUCATION

Within all divisions of college basketball, there are different types of academic institutions. You will need to know and understand these differences when choosing the college that's right for you. In the United States, people often call (what we in England call universities) "colleges" or "schools." So, when I say "state school or "college," I'm actually talking about a four-year college in the U.S. It's confusing, I know.

> ➤ **What is a state school?**

The term **state school** generally refers to schools funded by the state government. They are funded, in whole or in part, by public money, and tend to have a high enrollment. Some have as many as 50,000 students. For this reason, they also have large campuses and large class sizes. They tend to offer a broad curriculum, although some are known for their expertise in certain academic areas such as engineering, agriculture or education.

> ## What is a private school?

Unlike state schools, **private schools** in the U.S. are not run by the state or the governments. They retain the right to select their students and therefore are typically harder to get into than state schools. Most private schools are funded in whole or part by students' tuition, so they are usually more expensive as well. The aim of this how-to guide is to help you get a scholarship to fund you education, but's it's good to know that in general, students at private schools come from households with higher incomes.

> ## What is a liberal arts school?

A liberal arts school is a college that has a primary emphasis on undergraduate study in the liberal arts and sciences. Liberal arts teach a broad curriculum that encourages variety, creativity, free thinking and aims to prepare its students for an active part in civic life. In order to obtain a degree from a liberal arts college you'll be required to take courses in such disciplines as history, economics, mathematics, biology, and foreign language. You'll still declare a major, of course, but this is unlike the U.K. university system where you apply to one particular academic department and earn a specialized degree.

> ## What are my options: Do both public & private schools offer basketball scholarships?

Yes. Both public and private schools offer basketball scholarships. For the 2012-2013 academic year, there were 347 men's teams and 345 women's teams playing Division I basketball. For the men 233 (67%) of these were at public institutions and 114 (33%) were at private schools. This same year, there were nine conferences that were comprised of either all public or all private schools. The six conferences consisting of all public institutions were the Big Sky, Mid-American, Mountain West, Southwestern, Summit, and Western Athletic. The three conferences consisting of all private institutions were the Ivy, Metro Atlantic, and West Coast. Most conferences are a mix of public and private schools. [7]

If you look at the colleges some of our best U.K. players have attended, you will find a mixture of public and private institutions.

British Division I players who attended private colleges include: Tom Ward, St. Michaels College; Luol Deng, Duke University; Pops Mensu Bonsu, George Mason University; Ben Mockford, St. Francis College, New York.

British Division I players who attended public colleges include: Ashley Hamilton, Loyola Marymount University; Matthew Bryant Amaning, University of Washington; Ben Eves, University of Connecticut.

One major difference among colleges within the U.S. is how much money each school spends on intercollegiate athletics. For more than a century, in the U.S., sports have been deeply interwoven in the education system. And, as you might have picked up from our discussion on the financial aspects of the NCAA tournament, there is big money involved in college sports.

During every preseason (the time between arriving on campus and the first basketball game) while I was at Davidson College, our team would fly from Charlotte-Douglas International Airport near our campus to Austin, Texas, for a weekend of practice against the University of Texas to prepare for the upcoming season. The reason we bore the three-hour flight from North Carolina to Austin rather than scrimmage against a team closer to home was twofold: First, Davidson College coach Bob McKillop and University of Texas head coach Rick Barnes are long-time friends and former colleagues. In their formative coaching years, when they were both starting out, they coached together at Davidson College as volunteer assistants under the head coach at the time, Eddie Biedenbach. From this point, they each worked themselves up the coaching ladder into head coach positions at Division I basketball programs.

Second, the University of Texas is, year after year, one of the best basketball teams in the county. Hence, they are also one of the most lucrative teams in the country, netting a tidy $150 million in 2011 revenue. Compare this to Davidson's comparatively meager $3.5 million dollars of revenue (2011). The financial difference is most obvious in the programs' facilities. Davidson has an arena that seats 5,223. The University of Texas home court holds 16,734. In addition, they have multiple practice courts, a secluded dining area for the players to eat in, and an entire TV channel dedicated to University of Texas sports. It's crazy!

But does this monumental difference in financial backing stop little ol' Davidson College from competing with big bad

University of Texas on the hardwood? Not if Coach McKillop has anything to do with it. Basketball is particularly well-suited for schools looking to make a leap into greater national prominence. With only five starters, even a couple of great recruits can vault a program to national competitiveness and enable the team to make a deep run into the NCAA tournament.

U.S. HIGH SCHOOL: THE £5,000 CAVEAT

This book is designed to help you land a college scholarship, but there are a fair number of U.K. basketball players who have spent a year or more in a U.S. high school before transitioning to college. But if you are considering this route, proceed with caution. The first thing you need to find out is whether the prospective high school is public or private. This is important because it can affect the amount of financial aid available to you. Without going into too much detail, here's why:

There are limitations and requirements related to foreign (F-1) students attending public secondary/high schools (grades nine through 12). Under U.S. law, student F-1 visas cannot be issued to persons seeking to enter the United States in order to attend a public primary/elementary school or a publicly funded adult education program. F-1 student visas *can* be issued, however, to people who wish to attend a private high school. According to the Department of Homeland Security, foreign students who wish to attend public secondary school (high school) **must pay the full cost of education**. This fee is **mandatory** and cannot be waived. The law does not allow a student in F-1 status to attend public secondary school without paying tuition. The full, unsubsidized per capita (for each student) cost of education is the cost of providing education to each student in the school district where the public school is located; thus, the cost will vary depending on the state and possibly the county within that state. This amount is listed under "tuition" on the student's **Form I-20**[i]. If the Form I-20 does not include the cost of tuition, the student must have a notarized statement, signed by the designated school official (DSO) who signed the Form I-20, stating the full cost of tuition, and that the student has paid the tuition in full. Costs normally range between $3,000 and $10,000 (£1,862 and £6,200). This is a lot to take in but it essentially means that it is possible to attend and play basketball at a public high school but you must pay your own way.[8]

However, nothing in the law prevents an organization or an individual from paying the full tuition costs *for the student* as long as the payment does not come from public funds. The student must still show that he or she has sufficient funds to cover education and living expenses while in the United States. In most cases, unless you or your family are capable of paying the cost of public education outright, this is not a feasible option for you.

I found out these rules the hard way. In 2006, I attended a basketball camp in the Pocono Mountains in the U.S. and shortly after I returned, I came into contact with a public high school in Maine that was eager to have me come and play for its basketball

---

[i] The Form I-20 is a document issued by SEVP-certified schools (colleges, universities, and vocational schools) that provides supporting information on a student's F or M status

team. I was in communication with the coach and even a host family that lived near the school. My mum and I had had several phone calls with the family and we thought everything was falling into place. I put a lot of time and effort into setting myself up with a host family but all my efforts were for nought when I found out I would have to pay the full cost of tuition. Why did no one tell me this before? Why didn't the coaches warn me? Because they didn't know!

After reading this guide you will know more about the rules and regulations that regulate foreign student athletes than 95 percent of all college and high school coaches out there. So graciously accept their advice, but always make sure you follow up on any information you receive by doing your own research.

The second barrier to entry into a U.S. high school for foreign students is the limit on the amount of time you are able to stay and study at a U.S. high school. Secondary school attendance is limited to **12 month**s for students on F-1 visas. [9]

FINDING A COLLEGE: YOUR HOME AWAY FROM HOME

College might be among your life's most transformative years. It's an opportunity to really discover your strengths and weaknesses, who *you* are and what you're passionate about. It's a chance to be challenged, not coddled. But choosing a university can be a mind-boggling experience, especially in the U.S. There are 2,618 accredited universities in the United States, compared with only 166[10] in the United Kingdom.[11] Don't be scared to step outside your comfort zone and pick schools that look different and unusual. But how do you learn about the schools out there? Let's rely on our trusty friend *Google* for this one.

The Internet is the best place to find out about prospective schools. First, check out the college's mission statement and philosophy. Geographical location is also important. In the United Kingdom you can't drive more than around ten hours (in any direction) without plunging your car off a cliff and into the sea. In the United States, you can drive uninterrupted for days before you have to hit the brakes. New York to Los Angeles is more than 2,500 miles as the crow flies; that's almost as far as London is to New York. If you were to pick-up the entire United Kingdom and lay it on top of the U.S. east coast, you would see that it covers only three or four of the U.S.'s fifty states. Indeed, if one excludes Scotland and Wales, England fits nicely within the boundaries of the state of North Carolina.

This is why you need to factor in geography when planning for college in the U.S. The U.S. has 2,959,064 square miles of land, consists of 50 states; four different time zones; the Rocky Mountains; the Great Lakes; the Midwest's Tornado Alley; active volcanoes, alligator-filled swamps, arid deserts and stretches of luscious beach as far as the eye can see. The west coast of the States is almost twice as far from the U.K. as the east coast. Flight time from London Heathrow to New York is about 8.5 hours (the return flight is a little shorter because of the tailwinds) while a trip from London to Los Angeles, California, will take 11.5 hours.

The breadth of the U.S. across the globe means that it encompasses a lot of different climates, from humid continental in the north to humid subtropical in the south. Students at the University of Miami enjoy 12 months of summer while Boston University students endure six months of winter. Not to say one is better than the other, but make sure you do your research and know what you're in for. You need to know whether to pack a fur coat or flip flops.[ii]

TODAY'S TO DO'S

Now it's your turn to do some due diligence. Find a Web site that will help you choose a college or university in the U.S. A good website will allow you to search, at the very least, by type of college and state. Once you have chosen several schools that stand out to you, make sure they are an NCAA member school so you have the opportunity of getting a basketball scholarship. Create a list of the colleges you like. You will use this list when you fill out your 'prospect tracker' in the next chapter. Here are some useful links to get you started:

Finding the Right College for You
  ➢ www.myfuturecollege.com
  ➢ www.50states.com/college

List of NCAA Member School
  ➢ www.ncaa.com/schools/

[ii] Travelling twice as far by plane does not necessarily mean it will take twice as long. Flight paths, jet streams, and even the earths rotation can affect flight time.

(3)

Taking Action: What Can I do Today?

RECRUITMENT VS. SELF-PROMOTION

Flow with whatever is happening and let your mind be free.
Stay centered by accepting whatever you are doing.
This is the ultimate.

— CHUANG TZU

Recruiting is the term used to describe the process college coaches employ to search for prospective student-athletes to add to their rosters. Every basketball player wants to be recruited, but British players can have a particularly tough time in the process. The greatest disadvantage English players have compared to their U.S. counterparts is the 3,000 miles of Atlantic Ocean separating the U.K. and the U.S. How are you going to get recruited when you live so far away? Here's how: you'll get creative.

Meeting the Silver Fox and The Legend
of Billy "Beener" Hungrecker

"I'll be wearing a black suit and yellow tie," said Coach McKillop in his last email before arriving in the U.K. Coach McKillop's train was scheduled to arrive at York train station at 1 PM. The first time I contacted Coach McKillop was several weeks beforehand when I had sent him an A4 size envelope. The envelope contained a letter stating that I was interested in playing basketball for him at Davidson College. It also included a list of my stats (basketball and physical), a list of my academic achievements as well as a couple of references from my basketball coaches and one of my teachers. Finally, and most importantly, I enclosed a highlight DVD protected by a thin plastic case. The envelope, lined with bubble wrap, was then sealed with a strip of sellotape and posted to the United States.

On April 16, 2007, I received a brief email back from McKillop. In summary, it said, "Please send more game footage." The next morning I called my English coach and told him what had happened. At the time I was playing for Division 4 team Leeds Met Carnegie. I asked my coach for all the game footage we had. That night I stayed up into the early morning hours editing game footage on my laptop. Within 48 hours of receiving McKillop's email, I had posted a second DVD I felt confident in. Another couple of weeks passed before I received another email from McKillop. It said: "your DVD further piqued my interest. I would like to arrange a time to come to England and see you play in person." After a few more email exchanges, McKillop and I had arranged a date and time to meet. I couldn't wait for McKillop's arrival.

At the time I was studying at the University of York in Yorkshire. Under NCAA recruiting guidelines, McKillop had to watch me play at my university and not for my club team. With this news, I had reached my first hurdle. I had an internationally-renowned basketball coach coming to watch me play, and I had to get 10 players together for a game of pickup, something my university typically struggled to do. So I had to do some recruiting of my own. I had played a couple of games for my university team and had come to know some of the guys, but even with them, I still needed more bodies. I made flyers asking people to come and play pickup on a Saturday afternoon for a couple hours at the university sports center. I told them I had a scout coming to see me play and asked them to bring a couple of pounds to help cover the court hire. I hoped that if I told them what was at stake they wouldn't bail out at the last minute. The last thing I wanted was for McKillop to travel all the way from the United States only to find we didn't even have enough players for a game of 5 vs. 5. After sending this flyer to every person at the university over 6 feet tall, I had 11 people confirmed. Providing they actually showed up, I was all set. The only thing I had to do now was make sure McKillop arrived safely.

Over the years of playing basketball in Sussex and much of southeast England, I had developed a great friendship with a man called Billy Hungrecker. Billy was an American who grew up playing basketball in New Jersey. Given the nickname "Beener", Billy was a small, un-athletic white kid with dark shaggy hair. By appearance you wouldn't have thought that Billy was any good at basketball. However, first impressions were quickly replaced by feelings of awe and respect once Billy stepped on the court. Billy was athletic, skilled and wonderfully crafty. As he moved about the court, you saw an outstanding shooter with the ability to spot up for open shots or take his man off the dribble. Billy spent almost every second of every day working on his game—and it showed. Billy grew up in New York and spent most of his childhood days playing driveway basketball with other kids in the neighborhood. As Billy's game improved, he began playing in competitive leagues and soon became well-known around New Jersey's summer leagues. He was eventually discovered by Glen Gondrezick at a Jersey Shore game. After the game, and excited by his find, Gondrezick got straight on the phone and called University of Nevada-Las Vegas (UNLV) head coach Jerry Tarkanian (also known as "Tark the Shark", and one of the most successful coaches in college basketball history) and recommended Billy. But Billy ended up going to Temple University for his freshman year—he even won the 1976 Temple dunking contest as a freshman. He stayed at Temple for two seasons before transferring to UNLV to play under Tarkanian from 1979-1980.

In 1984, shortly after completing his college basketball career, Billy moved to England to play professional basketball for the Worthing Thunder. A prolific scorer in college, Billy found ways to be even more of an offensive threat as a pro. I remember his telling me about many of his scoring records, but none was more impressive than the 73 points he poured in against a strong Plymouth side at the Worthing Leisure center, as his team capped the season with an unbeaten 18-0 record. Billy's life was driven by the game of basketball and he continued to play professionally in England as long as his tiring body would allow. After his playing days finally came to an end, he became a youth coach in Sussex. This is how I met Billy; it was around 2001. He could see my passion for the game and knew it was my goal to play basketball in the U.S. He became great friends with my family and would drive by my house nearly every day to leave the *USA Today* newspaper on the kitchen counter so I could read the NBA box scores when I came home from school. He was committed to helping me live out my dream, and when he heard that McKillop (who grew up not far from him in New York City), would be visiting me in York, there was nothing stopping him from making the six-hour drive to be there in person.

So there we were, Billy and me standing on the main platform of York train station, on the lookout for a man in a black suit and yellow tie. I will never forget seeing Coach McKillop for the first time. He commands a large presence for a man with modest physical stature. He appeared to us striding down the platform out of a cloud of smoke—or that's how I remember it. After we said our "hellos" we took a five-minute taxi ride from the train station to the university sports complex. Billy was obviously excited to have someone from his neck of the woods to talk with—and the two gabbed in the back of the taxi for most of the ride. For Billy this was a rare treat of nostalgia. Once we arrived we headed straight for the sports hall where we sat on a bench and exchanged small talk for a moment before I excused myself and went to the changing rooms to put on my playing gear.

When I returned, I had to deal with many things English basketball players have become accustomed to. I'm sure you won't have any trouble picturing the following scene: my teammates and I wheeling off the badminton nets, sweeping dried mud off the court that probably came off someone's astro-boots, one of my teammates actually playing in astros, at least one person playing in a premiership football shirt, and too many pairs of Umbro socks to count. And of course all of this was taking place on a court that looked like a map of the London

Underground. For you and me, this is a typical day of English basketball. But for a Division I basketball coach who would go on to win a Bob Cousy Award[1], coach a nationally-ranked basketball team, appear in the NCAA Elite Eight, and coach the USA U20 National team, I'm sure he was wondering if he was watching the right sport. Yet, despite the quirks of the British game, I played like a stud, draining threes in transition, dunking in traffic, handling the ball and catching and finishing a perfectly placed lob pass. I was able to exhibit skill, strength, athleticism and basketball IQ. I couldn't have asked more from my university friends who had come out and played. The session lasted about an hour and a half and when it finally came to an end, Billy called a taxi to take McKillop back to the train station. Before he left, McKillop told me that he would go back to the U.S. and discuss what he had seen with his assistant coaches and be back in touch with me within a couple of weeks. Sure enough, just two weeks later Mckillop called me up and offered me a full ride scholarship to play basketball at Davidson College.

I couldn't have asked for more out of my freshman year. We finished the season 20-0 in the Southern Conference and made a deep run in the NCAA postseason tournament before losing in the Elite Eight to the eventual National Champions, the Kansas Jayhawks. We ended the season ranked as the 9th best team in the country. At the beginning of the following season,even after losing our senior class, we were ranked in the nation's top 25.

Davidson College was written in the headlines across the world.

And so was the name of the man I had met, wearing the yellow tie standing on the train platform, just a year previously. McKillop was named 2008 National Coach of the Year by the National Association of Basketball Coaches. He received the Coach Clair Bee Award. The same year, McKillop was selected to head the 2008 USA Basketball Men's U18 National Team that competed in the 2008 FIBA Americas U18 Championship in Formosa, Argentina.

He's been Southern Conference Coach of the Year eight times. Davidson has won 10 of the last 15 Southern Conference Division championships (seven of the last nine)and four of the last five league titles.

Note: Billy, a true basketball legend, passed away July 26, 2011. He called me from the U.K. every week during my college career to see how I was doing and to offer me advice. RIP, Billy. You are truly missed.

This is just part of my recruiting story. I could tell you a handful of similar stories that didn't end with a scholarship offer or show you a hundred emails that were sent to college coaches with no reply. It is important to hear the stories of how successful athletes made it to the top, but it's even more important to hear the stories of those who failed along the way, and why. This will broaden your perspective and make you realize that a scholarship offer is achievable only through hard work, persistence, and the ability to cope with rejection and move forward.

CREATING YOUR BASKETBALL CV

It's time to create your basketball **curriculum vitae (CV)**. Traditionally, a CV is a brief account of a person's education, qualifications, and previous experience. It's what most people use to apply for a new job. Using the same concept, you can use it to apply for a basketball scholarship. Most college recruiting is done in local high schools but some colleges will go to extreme lengths and travel great distances in hopes of finding the next Lebron James or Kobe Bryant. Once a college coach hears of a player he might like to add to his roster, he will go in search of game footage. If he likes what he sees on film, the coach, or one of his scouts will attend one of the player's high school games. If still interested, the next step would be to extend an invitation for the player to visit the college campus, meet the team, and get a feel for the place. This is called an **'official visit'** (we will talk more about 'official visits' in a moment). But let's back up a little.

The first thing you need to do is to get a college coach to come see you play. And although coaches do tend to roam beyond their U.S. borders, you cannot rely on their coming to you. You have to put yourself in front of them. This is what you call **self-promotion**. You have to sell yourself just like an auto dealer sells a car. It's all about show and tell. You need to *tell* him how good you are on paper (or email) and *show* him using a **highlight DVD**. The purpose of the highlight DVD is twofold:

1. **SEEING IS BELIEVING**. Showcasing your skill on film is the next best thing to having a college coach watch you in person.

2. **COVERING GROUND**. It's easy to copy a DVD and send it to a large number of potential schools. Capturing your skills on film

will allow you to be in more than one place at a time. We're looking for maximum exposure.

It's unlikely that you'll receive a scholarship offer based on a highlight DVD alone, but it's your best opportunity to get a foot in the door. In a lot of cases, a coach will make the decision to pursue you as a recruit—or take you off the list—based on your highlights; therefore the DVD is a vital part of the recruiting process.

CREATING A HIGHLIGHT DVD

Your highlight DVD is your first impression, so it has to be great. First, you'll need game tape to edit. If you do not have game footage already, make sure you record all of your upcoming games. Borrow or rent a camcorder and have a coach, family member, or friend work the camera during your games. When you're satisfied that you have enough good game footage to work with, you will need to start editing it on your computer. Basketball coaches in the U.S. are used to watching hundreds and hundreds of highlight DVDs every offseason. Just like books are organized from beginning, to middle, to end, highlight DVDs should follow a similar structure. In a book it would seem odd if you found the contents page at the end, and the same sort of thing applies to DVDs. This will make it easier for coaches to watch your DVD and evaluate your skills. Just follow these four simple steps:

STEP 1: Collect Game Footage

"Did you get that on camera?" We all know the feeling when you make a half court circus shot and spin around to see if anyone caught it on camera. By the same token, you never know when you are going to play your best game. Kobe Bryant said he felt tight before he scored 61 points against the Knicks in 2009. Don't risk *not* filming every game. I realize that every one of Kobe's games will be caught on camera from now until the day he dies, tight "hammy" or not, but you catch my drift.

STEP 2: Edit Your Footage

If you've never used a computer to edit video, , rest assured, it's easier than you may think. I won't go into detail about the steps of film editing but I will point you toward the right place to get started. Most of us work with either Windows or Apple operating software. If your computer has Windows operating software it comes preinstalled with **Windows Movie Maker**. Movie Maker is a freeware video-editing software by Microsoft. It is a part of the Windows Essentials software suite and offers the ability to create and edit videos. And if you have a Mac, you can use **iMovie**. iMovie is Apple's proprietary video-editing software application and typically comes preinstalled on Apple computers. iMovie imports video footage to the Mac using either the FireWire interface on most MiniDV-format digital video cameras or the computer's USB port. It can also import video and photo files from a hard drive. From there, you can edit the photos and video clips and add titles, music, and effects. Whether you're working with Windows or Apple software, both programs are more than capable of producing a killer highlight DVD.

DVD Structure

The first frame of your highlight DVD should be a static image, like a PowerPoint slide, that contains all of your vital information, including:

- ➢ name
- ➢ position (e.g., Guard, Power Forward, Center)
- ➢ height (feet and inches) & weight (pounds)
- ➢ hometown & nationality
- ➢ jersey number on the DVD
- ➢ contact details

It's important to place this frame at the start of the DVD and not the end because the recruiter might not watch the entire video. It's okay to include this frame again at the end as a reminder.

Live action highlights should be edited out of the footage and sorted into categories. Categories should include, and probably be limited to: scoring at the rim, outside shooting (jump shooting), post moves, rebounding, passing, and hustle plays. Don't underestimate the importance of the last category on this list. Coaches will chomp at the bit when they see a player sacrificing his body by diving out of bounds in pursuit of a loose ball or wrestling with the opponent for possession. You might want to include a static slide to introduce each section, but if you included a satisfactory number of highlights in each category, it should be obvious. After your highlights you will need to include a half-game of unedited footage, and not from just any game: your best half of basketball you've played this season.

Taking Action: What Can I do Today?

Should I include basketball drills on my highlight DVD?

It depends. If you were a player who had recently graduated from college and looking for a pro contract and you asked me the same question, I would say absolutely not. Pro teams expect you to have a considerable amount of experience and success in live action so that the players they sign can make an immediate impact on the court. College coaches, however, may base some of their decisions on a player's potential. For this reason it might be a good idea to add film of basketball drills. This is really up to you but most of your video highlights should be taken from an actual game.

STEP 3: Add Supporting Materials

Now that you have your highlights ready to burn onto a DVD you'll need to prepare some supporting materials to accompany your DVD. When being admitted to a college in the U.S. on an athletic scholarship, you are, first and foremost, a student. Remember that quote from the film, "*Coach Carter*"? The part where Samuel L. Jackson tells his team about prioritizing schoolwork and basketball: "In 'student-athlete,' 'student' comes first."Although cheesy, Samuel L. is right. You won't be able to play basketball in college unless you are a good student with good grades. Hence, you must use supporting materials to convince coaches that you are a good student and of sound character. This is the message you must get across in the supporting materials. You must include a **Cover Letter** and a **Reference**.

A good **cover letter** should be brief and to the point. You must convey enthusiasm for the sport and for the college. Make an honest assessment of your talent and write about your strengths and how you are ready to take your game to the next level. Don't be too modest. If you scored 50 points in a national league game, tell it to the coach! Base your cover letter on the template below.

Coach Krzyzewski,

My name is _____ and I am writing to you because I am interested in studying and playing basketball for you at _____ (college/university). I am a _____ (height) _____ (guard/forward/center) currently playing for _____ (club team) in the United Kingdom. I am a great athlete with a strong academic record and a passion for the game of basketball. I am ready and eager to make the transition to the college game and believe that your university will be the perfect fit. Please see below for a list of my athletic and academic achievements and also find enclosed my highlight DVD. Please feel free to contact me anytime at _____ (email address) or (phone number).

Athletic
6'6", 198lb
National Shield MVP
Great Britain U19
28 points, 10 rebounds in English Schools Final

Academic
GCSEs: 2A*, 3A's, 5B's, 1C
A levels: 2A's, 2B's

Thank you for your consideration. I look forward to hearing from you.

Ben Allison (Phone) (Email)

TWO THINGS EVERY COVER LETTER SHOULD CONTAIN

1. A CLEAR MESSAGE

State what you want to achieve. If you want a scholarship, say so. You have to make sure the coach knows that you want to play basketball at HIS or HER university and none other. Make it personal and write the name of the university in the email. Don't take shortcuts and send a cookie-cutter letter to a bunch of colleges with "Dear Sir" or "Dear Madam." Use the coach's name and the name of the university. When you put in the time and do your research, this will show in the letter.

2. A CALL-TO-ACTION

What do you want the coach to do after he or she watches your highlight DVD? Make sure your cover letter has a strong **call-to-action**. A call-to-action is a message that tells the coach what to do next. In this instance, the best call to action is "Please call me or email me." If you are going to be in the United States and close to the college, let the coach know. Remember, it's all about self-promotion.

The second thing to include is a **reference** from your basketball coach or a teacher at your school. A reference is a written statement from a person who can vouch for your qualities and strengths. It needs to be only a paragraph or two, but it will help lift your credibility in the eyes of the coach.

STEP 4: Mail Your DVD

Now you have your package with your highlight DVD and supporting materials. But where do you send it? This will become clearer as you research more and get an idea of the different colleges and playing options available. But, as with most things in life, the more the better.

I have created a "prospect tracker" to help you select colleges to which you'll send highlight DVDs. The tracker also helps you track their responses.

PROSPECT TRACKER: HOW IT WORKS

Initially, send out about 12 packages to a combination of Division I and Division II private and public colleges. Take a look at the Prospect Tracker below. The 12 colleges will be made up of three private and three public colleges at both Division I and Division II levels. These 12 packages will be your first wave of DVDs. The response rate will vary depending on your abilities and the types of schools you apply to. If you send out 12 DVD packages and get replies from three schools that show interest in you, you're response rate is 25 percent. This isn't a bad, however you should aim for a response rate of about 40 percent. Packages sent to the United States can take up to two weeks to arrive, so give college coaches three to four weeks to reply. By this time, if your response rate is below the 40 percent target, think about changing your strategy. This could involve sending follow-up emails, calling the coach directly, or changing the type of schools you are applying to. If you aren't getting a response from the bigger schools, try smaller ones. If you aren't getting any response from Division I schools, send a follow-up email to see if they have received your DVD and request feedback from their evaluation. Don't get discouraged if it seems like you're talking to the world but no one is listening. At the end of the day, all you need is one scholarship offer to make it all worthwhile. Hang in there.

PROSPECT TRACKER

Division I Colleges

	Head Coach	Email Address	Phone Number	Response
Private	1. John Smith	jsmith@college.edu	(847) 202 XXXX	
	2.			
	3.			
	4.			
	5.			
Public	1.			
	2.			
	3.			
	4.			
	5.			

Division II Colleges

	Head Coach	Email Address	Phone Number	Response
	1.			
	2.			
	3.			
	4.			
	5.			
	1.			
	2.			
	3.			
	4.			
	5.			

Sloppiness is a Disease

Has anyone ever told you that you have to develop good habits? It's usually your mother telling you to say "please and thank you," "brush your teeth" or "tidy your room." We call these good habits because they are tasks that should be completed on a daily basis to maintain a healthy lifestyle. A habit is an acquired pattern of behavior followed regularly until it has become almost involuntary. At first, remembering to pick your clothes up off the floor or brush your teeth is hard. But the more you do it, the easier it becomes until it's second nature. It's the same on the basketball court. In basketball, good habits win games. Boxing out should be a habit. Running the court should be a habit. Having a hand in the passing lane should be a habit. Running to help up a teammate should be a habit. But having good habits is a skill you need to develop on and off the court. I have come to know that you can't have one without the other.

How can you have the discipline to rebound on every possession when you aren't disciplined enough to clean up after yourself at home? When you don't develop good habits in life, people will start to call you sloppy or lazy. My coach used to say, "Sloppiness is a disease." He would say it in practice when we gave up on a play or he would write it on the whiteboards when we left a mess in the locker room. He believed that sloppiness was a disease that would spread uncontrollably through your life if you let it. It would also spread to others, especially the younger guys on the team. If they saw you give up on a play then they will think it's okay to do the same. To be detailed and to develop good habits on the basketball court, you need to include the same type of discipline in every part of your life. Take hold of your own life and be an example for others.

I make this point because in emails and letters sent to college coaches, I see a lot of "sloppiness" in the form of spelling mistakes and grammatical errors. When a college coach sees this, it looks like you don't care. Make sure you take the time to proofread all your emails and cover letters to college coaches and recruiters.

Things may come to those who wait, but only the things left by those who hustle.

— ABRAHAM LINCOLN

Be Aggressive

In the recruiting process, it's your responsibility to make regular follow-ups with the coach. You cannot wait by the phone for coaches to call or expect scholarship offers to flow in through the letterbox. You have to take action. College coaches can telephone recruits starting June 15th at the conclusion of the student-athlete's sophomore year. This is basically the summer before you go to sixth-form college. However, there is no restriction on the time (or number of times) that you can call a college coach. Call coaches daily, follow up, and continue to send recruiting packets, even visit college campuses and arrange to meet with the coach if you have the means. Often, less-skilled high school basketball players can earn scholarships over more-talented players simply because they followed a plan to get recruited.

Be Persistent

If the first few coaches don't call you back or show much interest in what you have to offer, don't get discouraged—and whatever you do, don't quit. It might take two weeks to get picked up. It might take a year. The point is you must keep moving forward and stay on track during recruiting. Athletes who can do this will eventually be rewarded.

Work on your acting skills: Life is a performance

To be a great champion, you must believe you are the best.
If you're not, pretend you are

—MUHAMMED ALI

It was only five minutes into practice and Coach McKillop was about to blow a gasket. I had the ball and was trying to make a move to the basket. I made an unconvincing shot fake, took one side dribble and pulled up for a jump shot. Only thing was, my defender stayed right beside me. As I tried to release the ball at the top of my jump, in an arching parabola into the basket, he pummeled it, embarrassingly, into the first row of the stands.

"That's why you haven't been able to get a Davidson girl to go on a date with you! You can't act!" Coach McKillop began striding towards me from the sideline as he screamed this (somewhat inaccurate) insult until we were standing toe to toe, his face inches from mine. "Life is all about acting," he continued to scream at me. His uncomfortably-close proximity meant that I could now feel his spits of fire hitting my face. I was used to these encounters with coach McKillop (this wasn't the first time I'd messed up in practice) but I wanted to stop him and explain that I had accompanied at least two or three female classmates from the library to the student union during my time at

Davidson, which (by my standards) constituted at least one Davidson date. But I refrained and allowed McKillop to get his point across. Finally he turned away from me and I took a big gulp of air as I realized I had been holding my breath. He then addressed the entire team:

"Basketball is about acting. It's about make-believe. When you jab step, you have to act as if you are making a move to the basket. When you shot-fake, you have to act as if you are *actually* shooting the ball, causing your defender to leave his feet. If you don't have a good act, no one is going to believe you." McKillop paused to let his message resonate throughout the arena. Just like I was unable to convince my defender that I was going to shoot the ball with my shot fake, Coach McKillop was suggesting I was similarly unable to convince a girl to go out with me.

Practice went on and although McKillop's message kind of made sense, I didn't really think much more about it. It wasn't until I was sitting in an introductory anthropology class that I really had an AHA! moment. In the class the professor was talking about sexuality and gender. He posed the question, "what makes males and females different—aside from biological differences, of course?" When you're walking down the high-street how can you tell boys from girls, men from women, males from females? You can tell, he concluded, by the way they dress and by the way they behave. Women grow long hair and put on dresses. Men act *masculine* by appearing rugged, strong and stern. Just like an actor puts on a costume and performs on stage, 'everyday people' do the same from the moment they wake up till the time they go to bed. We dress and behave in a certain way so other people will make the correct judgment of us.

Taking Action: What Can I do Today?

You can use the art of performance to your advantage. Ever heard the phrase, "Dress for the job you want, not the job you have?" If you start to dress like the person you want to be, people will start to treat you that way. Similarly, if you step onto the basketball court with the confidence that you're the best player out there, people will treat you like that person. And you will soon find it to be a self-fulfilling prophecy. Fake it till you make it, my friends. This is a lesson I have been using regularly in my life after Davidson College.

In February 2012, after I had graduated from college, I applied for a job in advertising. Without a day of advertising experience under my belt, I was able to convince a company to pay me nearly $10,000,— on top of hiring fees and salary, for an entry-level position during a time the United States was emerging from its sixth successive quarter of negative economic growth, making it one of the worst economic recessions in U.S history. Salaries had been frozen. No one was hiring. College presidents were handing out diplomas, shaking hands and muttering a tentative— and slightly sarcastic "good luck"—before slinging their newly-birthed alumni out into an economy in crisis.[1]

How'd I do it? I performed. I acted as if I had a lot of advertising experience. I told stories that showed qualities necessary for the position. I hid my insecurities and apprehensions and interviewed with confidence. I put on a show and made this company believe that I was too valuable to pass up. Was I *really?* I don't know. But I wasn't going to leave it up to chance.

Official Visits

If a college coach is impressed with your highlight DVD, he or she may extend an invitation for an official visit to the college. The official visit is one of the more exciting tactics used by college coaches. Official visits are not given to just anyone—they're reserved for best of the best.

According to the NCAA, an official visit is "any visit to a college campus by you and your parents paid for by the college. The college may pay all or some of your expenses." These expenses can include transportation to and from the college, room and meals, and "reasonable entertainment expenses, including complimentary admissions to a home athletics contest." Per NCAA guidelines, for most sports, you can visit a school only once on an official visit and make official visits at only five Division I schools. You can make an unlimited number of official visits to Division II schools.

The NCAA's strict rules governing official visits help to protect both the recruit and the college. Official visits are usually the same among colleges around the States. With most visits, you will be on the campus for up to (and no more than) 48 hours and you will get in on every aspect of the college's life: checking out a practice or game, touring the campus, eating in the cafeteria, going to class, and joining in on the social atmosphere. You will usually be picked up from the airport by an assistant coach and driven straight to the basketball offices on campus to meet with the rest of the coaching staff. After meeting the coaches, you will then be introduced to your hosts, usually senior players on the basketball team who will give you a campus tour, manage your per diem, and essentially look after you during the visit. You will then go to dinner with the coaches and some of the players (on the first night). They are looking to impress you so you can usually order whatever you want from the menu. After dinner, the hosts will take you back to your accommodation and the night progresses from there. You almost always meet up with a few more team members, but nightly activities will vary. It can be laid back as staying in the apartment and playing video games, going to a movie, or going to a campus or fraternity party.

The NCAA allows the college to entertain you in the community where the college is located, but these must be scalable and comparable to normal student life. Davidson College, for example, is situated a couple of miles from Lake Norman. Lake Norman is the largest man-made lake in the United States, with 520 miles of shoreline. The college owns 110 acres of waterfront property that the students can enjoy. During the summers the lake campus is packed with students waterskiing, going on boat rides, or just enjoying a swim. During an official visit at Davidson College the recruit will typically start day two off with a boat ride— a great way to start any morning. The recruit and his/her hosts will leave from the Davidson Lake campus on a 25-minute boat ride to a dock outside the North Harbor café where they'll eat breakfast. Before the recruit departs on Sunday they will play pickup with the team. The coaches are not allowed to watch the pick-up session, according to NCAA rules. But, in the past couple of years, the NCAA introduced a rule that allows the coaches to work out the recruits while they are on campus for their official visit. If you do go to high school or prep school before going to college in the U.S., this is good information. In order to be as relaxed as possible on your visit it's good to know what to expect.

In addition to knowing what to expect from the college, be prepared to ask questions. Astute questions demonstrate an impressive level of interest in the athletic program and the coach. Here are a few examples to get you started:

➢ What is the team's travel schedule like? How does that factor into academics/school?

➢ Why do you see me as a good "fit" for this team? Would I be a starter? A walk-on? Are there already many athletes in my position, i.e., four guards and you would be the fifth—would that be worth it?

➢ How many athletes are being recruited for the team?

➢ What is the practice schedule like/how many hours per week?

➢ Is there practice in the off-season?

And lastly, enjoy it. It's a once (or five times) in a lifetime experience.[2]

Finding Competition in the Mountains

When I was 18 years old I was given a book to read by my basketball coach, Billy Hungrecker, called *The Miracle of St. Anthony* by Adrian Wojnarowski. It chronicles a season of the St. Anthony High School basketball team coached by the legendary high school coach Bob Hurley. But St. Anthony is not your run-of-the-mill high school and Bob Hurley is not your average coach. Coach Hurley has become a living legend within the basketball community across the United States; not just for his impressive win-loss record, but as well for the way in which he cares for his players and the community.

St. Anthony's is situated in a poor and drug-ridden corner of Newark, New Jersey. Coach Hurley makes sure that his players learn lessons that will help them in life on and off the court. It has been a long time since I read this book but there is one particular anecdote that has stuck with me. It was one where Hurley made sure that all his players had zippers sown into their tracksuit trouser pockets. It goes like this:

Rebook shipped sneakers [to the St. Anthony basketball team] twice in the preseason, and twice again in the regular season. They furnished the team with sweat suits and gave the coaches a modest clothing allowance to use with the company.

However, there was one thing about [the newest] shipment that Coach Hurley was displeased with:

The sweatsuit pants had no pockets.

He wasn't one of those high school coaches who wanted something in the pockets, just pockets.

"After practice, it's not like college where we're going up into our dorm rooms," Hurley explained. "We've all got bus fare, and we can't be walking around without pockets in our sweats. It's not like we need cars. We just need pockets for our sweat pants."[3]

Hurley's attention to detail and thoughtfulness for his players struck a chord with me. Coach Hurley's players were "the poorest of the poor" (more than 50% of the students' families lived below the poverty line). It's a tiny school, constantly on the edge of bankruptcy that's held together by a determined band of Felician nuns. His players didn't have cars outside and if they lost their change for the bus, they'd be walking home. Hurley's players were his family and he wouldn't want his family walking the Newark streets after dark.

After I read this book, I wanted in; I wanted to be part of a family of basketball players and coaches who had each other's backs. At the time I was attending a school similar to St. Anthony's. My school, Christ's Hospital School, wasn't run by Felician nuns but it was founded in 1554 by Prince George VI on principles of charity and benevolence, the same principles it relies on today.[i] I loved my time at Christ's Hospital but wanted to hold the same love for St. Anthony's School and its basketball program.

St. Anthony's is just like Christ's Hospital, but had the added bonus of a top-rated basketball program. So I did some research and found out that during the summer months, Bob Hurley ran his own

---

[i] Check out the school uniform I had to wear during high-school: http://en.wikipedia.org/wiki/Christ%27s_Hospital

basketball camp in the Pocono Mountains of Pennsylvania, located in the northeastern U.S. The Bob Hurley Basketball camp is organized by the Hoop Group, a well-known brand for basketball teaching across the U.S. I knew Bob Hurley would be there and would have the opportunity to see me play. It would also be a great chance to test my skills against the top U.S. players of my age.

I arranged to fly to New York City and spent a few days there getting settled. I visited the Statue of Liberty and the Metropolitan Museum of Art; I also caught a New York Yankees baseball game. After a couple of days taking in the Big Apple, I was ready to make my way to camp.

The Pocono Mountains are located in northeastern Pennsylvania, about a three-hour drive from New York. I booked a bus ticket to the camp, departing from Grand Central Station in Midtown Manhattan. I managed to get some much-needed sleep on the bus but soon arrived in the Poconos. The bus dropped me off at a small, unmanned bus station containing only a Coke machine, a pay phone and a few rows of vacant plastic chairs bolted to the tile floor. I used the pay phone to call a taxi, bought myself a drink and took a seat. The taxi soon arrived and we sped up the winding hills to the Pocono Mountains and the Bob Hurley basketball camp.

The U.S. can be intimidating. It's big, brash and loud. I was scared of the U.S. even before I stepped on the basketball court, heck, before I left the airport in NYC I was intimidated when I went through customs after arriving at John F. Kennedy airport. I was intimidated in a number of restaurants because I didn't know how to order. I was intimidated in the taxi on the way to the airport because I had no credit card, only a little bit of cash on me—and there were no cash machines for miles around. What if I didn't have enough money? But, as my college coach would later say, "you have to get comfortable being uncomfortable." This, he said, was the only way you were going to get better. I felt intimidated because I was outside of my comfort zone; I had put myself in a situation I hadn't been in before and my body was on edge. It's just like when you are really pushing yourself on the basketball court. Your body is feeling pain and discomfort because you are putting it through things that it has never experienced before. You are jumping higher, moving faster and enduring more that you ever have. It may not be pleasant at the time but your mind and body learn to cope, and the next time you find yourself in the same situation it won't be nearly as bad. You can smile and say, "been there, done that."

The camp is up high in the Pocono mountains and the only thing you can see 360 degrees around you is green grass and forest trees. It felt as though a grizzly bear would come strolling through the camp at any moment, looking for a human snack. All of the courts are outside and the campers sleep in wooden cabins that house around eight people each. I arrived at the camp a little late so I was shown to my cabin and told to change straight into my playing gear and make my way out to the courts.

Overall, I had a great experience. I had a fun week and the coaches selected me to the camp all-star team. I was by no means the best basketball player there and, at times, I felt like I was being bullied on the court. It was an extremely tough but necessary experience.

Bob Hurley was there every day of camp. He lectured the campers daily and could be seen walking around, observing, and chatting on the sidelines. Through word of mouth, coach Hurley knew I was interested in playing for him at St. Anthony's but he showed no interest in me. The camp ended, everyone began their journeys home, and I had no further contact with Bob Hurley or St. Anthony's after that. But, as they say, as one door closes, another one opens.

It just so happened that I wasn't the only English person who travelled from the U.K. to attend Hurley's camp. Drawn together by our brodgy English accents, I soon met Coach Matthew Newby. Coach Newby was a youth basketball coach in Yorkshire, in England, who travels to the U.S. every summer to coach at camps and clinics on the East Coast. Newby had brought several of his U18 players to the States to attend the camp and experience a bit of American culture. I quickly got to know Newby as a guy who was passionate about basketball. I started telling coach Newby a little bit about myself and what had brought me to the Poconos. He helped me talk through my options for playing basketball. At this time I had just finished my A2, the summer was drawing to a close and the new academic year was near. I didn't have any scholarship offers in the U.S. and didn't have many options, apart from accepting one opportunity I had been offered through UCAS at the University of York. Once I started to chat to Coach Newby and describe the options I had at hand he became excited. It turned out that he had been appointed head coach of Leeds Metropolitan Carnegie, a Division 4 men's team based out of Leeds Met Carnegie University. Leeds is a city about 45 minutes' drive west of York. If I accepted my place to study at the University of York, I'd be able to drive or take the train to Leeds to play for Newby. I wasn't too thrilled with the offer at the time but Newby and I swapped contact details nonetheless and parted ways.

I did, in fact, go back to the U.K. to study economics at the University of York and play basketball for Coach Newby and Leeds Met Carnegie. We became the Division 4 regular season champions and National Shield winners. I didn't get much exposure from playing in the lowly EBL Division 4 league but it was enough to get me a tryout for the Great Britain U20 team. I tried out at the Amechi Center in Manchester and made the GB U20 training squad in preparation for the summer European Championships in Poland.

Looking back, it's extremely ironic that I travelled all the way to the U.S. in hopes of an offer to play basketball Stateside, and the only offer I actually got was for a team back in England. All I can say is that opportunity lies in the most unpredictable places and sometimes you have to take a step backward in order to move forward.

DON'T UNDERSELL YOURSELF

Below is an excerpt from *The 4-Hour Workweek* by author Timothy Ferris:

It's lonely at the top. Ninety-nine percent of people are convinced they are incapable of achieving great things, so they aim for mediocre. The level of competition is thus fiercest for "realistic" goals, paradoxically making them the most time- and energy-consuming. It's easier to raise $10,000,000 than it is $1,000,000. It's easier to pick up the one perfect 10 in the bar than five 8s.

If you are insecure, guess what? The rest of the world is, too. Do not overestimate the competition and underestimate yourself. You are better than you think.

Taking Action: What Can I do Today?

Did you know that European players tend to be more fundamentally sound than American players? Professional players in Europe know that to succeed in Europe, they have to be able to make basketball plays. European teams don't hire guys who can't shoot or pass. American college and NBA teams, on the other hand, believe in specialization. One guy is a shooter, the next a rebounder, the other a shot-blocker. 7-foot-2 center Dikembe Mutombo is commonly referred to as one of the greatest shot-blockers of all time. He wasn't a great offensive player but he didn't need to be. Mutombo should be thankful that the NBA existed. He'd be making about £12 a year in Europe. So don't sell yourself short. If you think you can't make it because you are lacking in a particular area of your game, just think of Dikembe Mutombo.

TOOLS & TRICKS

International Phone Calls

➢ **Skype (www.skype.com)**
Free internet calls and cheap, easy international calling.
➢ International Calling Guide: www.hoetocallabroad.com/usa

Making Your Highlight DVD

➢ **How Video Editing Works:** www.howstuffworks.com/video-editing
➢ **How to Burn a DVD:** www.wikihow.com/Burn-a-DVD

Notable U.S. Basketball Camps

➢ **Hoop Group:** www.hoopgroup.com (732) 502-2255

The Hoop Group hosts camps and clinics, providing expert instruction, competition and exposure to amateur players.

➢ **5 Star Basketball Camp:** www.fivestarbasketball.com

The most prestigious basketball camp in the country that boasts an impressive list of camp alumni and coaching staff. This camp attracts the top U.S. high school recruits and guarantees top competition.

➢ **East Coast Invitation:** (336) 983-2099

4

Applying to College—the American Way

TAKING THE SAT (SCHOLASTIC ASSESSMENT TEST)

If the college you visit has a bookstore filled with t-shirts rather than
books, find another college.
—R. ALBERT MOHLER JR.

College has given me the confidence I need to fail.
—JAROD KINTZ

Even if you have been offered a college basketball scholarship, you will still have to go through the college admission process, the equivalent of the UCAS system in the U.K. Part of the admissions process is sitting for the **Scholastic Assessment Test (SAT)**. Nearly every college admissions department in the United States will require you to take the SAT, a standardized test that's owned, published and developed by the **College Board**. It tests your knowledge of reading, writing, and math. The critical reading section includes passages and sentence completions. The writing section includes a short essay and multiple-choice questions where you identify errors and improve grammar and usage. Finally, the mathematics section includes questions on arithmetic operations, algebra, geometry, statistics and probability. To prepare for the test and achieve a good score, it's vital that you plan ahead.

The first step of planning ahead should be to register for the SAT. Even before you have any interest from potential U.S. colleges, it's a good idea to go ahead and register for the test because you can only take it on certain dates. Just like your GCSEs or A-levels, the SAT is administered by an examination board (e.g., AQA) so you can't just take the test whenever you like. Most college application deadlines are between November 30th and February 28th, depending on the school. Most U.S. high-schoolers take the SAT twice—once in the spring of their junior year (lower 6th form) and again in the fall or their senior year (upper 6th). I suggest that you stay on the same schedule. Keep in mind that you must have completed the SAT before your college applications are due. If you take the SAT in May or June of your last year or 6th form, it will be too late if you wish to enroll in college for the following academic year. These dates are for people who are taking the SAT early during their AS year.

Part of your registration for the exam will be choosing a **SAT testing center**. The SAT is normally held at college or university campuses that serve as testing centers. The SAT is always held at a London location and in a few other major U.K. cities. Testing centers *do* change from year to year, so to be certain, check the College Board Web site (http://sat.collegeboard.org/) to find the testing center closest to you. This may sound obvious, but make sure you have clear directions to the testing center to use on the day of the test. You want to be as relaxed as possible, and getting lost before the test will add extra anxiety to your day.

I took the SAT twice before I made my way the U.S. and the second time I did significantly better than the first. *Note: The word "retake" in the U.K. can have negative connotations. If you are retaking one of your examinations, people may think you messed up. Not in the U.S. Retaking the SAT more than once is encouraged, as you will be sending only your best scores to colleges as part of your application.*

The second time, I knew what to expect and felt more relaxed and confident. The test is 3 hours and 45 minutes long and consists mainly of multiple choice questions. The seemingly endless string of questions can get tedious, but it is important that you don't lose focus and lapse into a **response set**. A response set is the tendency of test-takers to respond systematically to questions on a test, regardless of content. For instance, a test-taker may select only (a) as the answer to every multiple-choice question, instead of reading the question and trying to figure out the correct answer by using logic and reasoning. Some people foolishly believe that this tactic will get them a decent score. This strategy will not work. If you give in to the temptation to cheat the system, you're setting yourself up to fail. The only way to do well on this test is to familiarize yourself with the test format and to answer practice questions. Familiarity with the test and each of its sections will help you track your progress and manage your time effectively. And, as basketball players, we all know what a little practice can do!

If you are the type of person who gets restless easily, then take steps to help you relax. Getting restless in a lesson or an exam is very annoying. One half of you is trying to concentrate, while the other half of you is dying for exercise, resulting in fidgeting and an overall lack of concentration. Try walking around before the test begins but make sure you are always in earshot of the testing room in case you are called in. If you think it will help, exercise or work out the day before the exam. Go down to your local gym and put up some shots. Just think about taking steps to clear your head before the exam.

At the end of the day, the SAT should be treated the same as any GCSE or A-level examination. Good practices include getting a good night's sleep the night before and having a good breakfast the morning of. The last thing you want is to feel hungry, thirsty or fatigued during the exam. It's a long test and you need to maintain a steady head. Lastly, make sure you don't drink too many fluids right before you're called in! Below are some of the lesser-known tips for SAT test-taking.

10 SAT TEST-TAKING TIPS

1. **Answer easy questions first.** You don't get extra points for answering correctly the harder questions, so don't waste your time trying to work them out. Remember the order of difficulty. In each section of the SAT (apart from the critical reading section), the questions start out easy and become increasingly difficult. The obvious answers at the beginning of a section may

be correct. Get through the easiest part of the SAT first, before attempting the hard questions.

2. **Use process of elimination.** Wrong answers are usually easier to find. Unless you are working on a particularly difficult question, usually you can rule out one or more answers. You are penalized one quarter point when you get a question wrong on the SAT, so answer the question only when you can eliminate other answers. If you are going to guess, guess smart.

3. **Know when to skip a question.** Sometimes after reading a question, you know that you will not be able to come up with an answer. Leave the question blank if you can't eliminate at least one wrong choice. Rather than spending 10 minutes trying to narrow down your choices, skip the question. If you have time at the end, you can go back and have another go at it.

4. **Use your test book.** Write in the test booklet. Use it to write down math equations. Outline, paraphrase, and underline to help you work through problems and identify correct answers. It's perfect for scratch work. Cross off eliminated answers, make notes, and mark off questions that you have skipped so you can easily reference them later.

5. **Keep track of time.** Sounds easy, right? Not always. In the heat of the moment, it is easy to lose track of time. Sometimes it's best to slow down. It's difficult to answer all the questions and

maintain accuracy. Answering a few questions correctly is better than guessing at the entire lot.

6. **Transfer answers at the end of each section**. This will save you time flipping back and forth between your worksheet and the scantron sheet.[i] Double check your answers. If you have time make sure you didn't skip a question from the test booklet and forget to skip the same question on the scantron, putting your answers out of sync.[1]

7. **Don't second-guess yourself**. Statistics prove that your first answer is usually correct, so follow your gut.

8. **Take a spare pencil**. And a second spare!

9. **Take practice tests ahead of time**. You're a basketball player. You know the benefits of good practice. There are free practice test questions on the College Board website. You must practice questions from every section to gain familiarity with the section structure. Reading section instructions during the test, if you didn't practice and familiarize yourself with the question types, will waste a lot of your time and could hurt your overall score. The other thing you have to remember is that you will most likely be studying for and taking the SAT around the same time as your English GCSE or A-level examinations. Making sure you schedule enough time to study for both requires forward thinking and good time management.

---

[i] **Scantron Sheet** is an answer sheet for multiple-choice testing.

10. Remember to relax[2] Take a deep breath and try to relax. Hey, what's the worst that can happen?

SAT: How'd I Do?

The table below shows the average test scores across all test-takers in 2012. This information *is* useful; however, it makes more sense to compare your scores with the averages of those admitted to the colleges you are applying. This way you will get a better idea of your chances of being accepted.

Test Section	Average Score
Critical Reading	496
Mathematics	514
Writing	488

Table Showing Average SAT Scores for the Class of 2012

Just like in the U.K., admittance to university is extremely competitive. According to the "2012 State of College Admissions" report published by the National Association for College Admission Counseling, the odds of any one student being accepted to any one college of your choice are approximately 2 out of 3, in your favor.[3] This means that if you averaged absolutely *all* college acceptance rates nationally, *including* Ivy League colleges,[ii] all the way down to good old Podunk State U., the national average college acceptance rate is 67 percent. However, this is the average across all schools in

---

[ii] The Ivy League is a collegiate athletic conference composed of sports teams from eight elite private institutions of higher education in the Northeastern United States. Harvard, Priceton and Yale are all Ivy Leage colleges.

the U.S. The top schools can have an acceptance rate as small as eight to 10 percent. To find the acceptance rates and the average SAT scores for the schools you're applying to, go to the college's Web site and check the admissions section.

Submitting SAT Scores

Your SAT scores can be sent straight to the colleges of your choice online through the College Board Web site. Every time you register for the SAT you get to send your results to four colleges of your choice for free; however, the colleges must be specified at registration or within nine days of taking the test. You'll have to pay an additional fee to have your scores sent to more than four schools. There's a good chance this will happen because you probably won't have your list of schools finalized by the time you take the test. Once you have your SAT scores, you are ready to complete the rest of your application.

CAN I HAVE AN APPLICATION, PLEASE?

"I'm not telling you it is going to be easy, I'm telling you it's going to be worth it."

—ART WILLIAMS, PRO BASKETBALL PLAYER

The **Common Application** is an undergraduate admissions application that applicants may use to apply to any of 488 member colleges and universities in the United States. The common application makes the admissions process a lot easier because you don't have to complete a ton of totally different applications. It's designed around a holistic admissions process that includes essays, recommendations and such secondary school information as **class rank** and SAT scores. The application can be filled out and submitted online so you can avoid postage costs. The majority of U.S. colleges will accept the common application but most will ask for a few additional materials like questionnaires, short answer questions, essays, and cover letters. So be prepared.

College Application Fees & Fee Waivers

Colleges charge around $50-$80 (£30-£50) per application,[4] payable by credit card online. Most schools have a fee waiver for students from low-income families. While in England, I went to a private secondary school for children from lower-income households that educates a portion of its students free of charge, and most at a reduced rate. This made me eligible for a college application fee waiver. To get my U.S. college application fees waived I asked the school headmaster to write a brief letter that described my financial situation. I made sure it was signed and stamped with the school seal to make it look official and sent it along with my application. I had no real idea what I was doing, but it seemed to do the trick. If you [don't] ask, you shall [not] receive. If you think you are eligible for a fee waiver or are truly struggling to afford the application fees, have your school's registrar or bursar write a brief letter describing your financial situation and include it with your application.

TOOLS & TRICKS

The SAT

- ➤ **SAT Home:** www.sat.collegeboard.org

- ➤ **SAT Testing Centers:** www.sat.collegeboard.org/register

- ➤ **International Students & the SAT:**
  professionals.collegeboard.com/testing/international/sat

- ➤ **SAT Test Dates & Deadlines:**
  professionals.collegeboard.com/testing/sat-reasoning/

SAT Practice

- ➤ www.sat.collegeboard.org/practice

Free sample practice questions and affordable practice tools.

The Common Application

- ➤ **The Common Application Homepage:**
  www.commonapp.org/Login

⑤

Applying for a Visa (Not the Credit Card!)

JUMPING THROUGH HOOPS OF FIRE: THE VISA APPLICATION

A journey of a thousand miles must begin with a single step.

– LAO TZU

If you're not living on the edge, you're taking up too much space.

— ANONYMOUS

Congratulations! You've been accepted to a prestigious U.S. college on a full basketball scholarship. Now you just need the documentation that will grant you access to your extended stay in the States. Namely, an F-1 student visa.

The main purpose of your visit to the United States is to study, so you will be applying for a student visa. They call this an F-1 student visa and it will be issued by the U.S. Department of Homeland Security. Getting an F-1 visa can be surprisingly easy. In 2012, 447,385 F-1 student visas were issued, so you are not alone. The visa process is centered around an interview with an embassy representative who has the final say on whether your visa is approved or denied. Once you a have been accepted to a U.S. college, you will need to follow a few simple steps.

➢ **BEFORE THE INTERVIEW**

Step 1   Complete the online visa application (DS-160) that permits you to apply for a visa to enter and study in the U.S. Put "Does Not Apply" for any information pertaining to American residents and citizens, such as Social Security Number and Taxpayer Identification Number.

Step 2   Your U.S. school or university will send you a form confirming that you have been accepted at an institution authorized by the **U.S. Citizenship and Naturalization Service** to enroll non-immigrant students (the **I-20** for an F-1 visa). You will read and sign this form. Make sure you complete this form more than 48 hours before your embassy appointment.

Step 3   Pay your SEVIS fee (U.S. $200, explained on p. 94) online through the Form I-901 application. Here you need to fill out the I-901 form (important information includes the school code, your SEVIS number both printed on the I-20 form) and pay the fee using a credit card. Print the receipt for your records. You may also pay this fee by mailing a money order to the Department of Homeland Security or using Western Union's Quick Pay Service.

Step 4   Make the interview appointment and pay the U.S. $160 visa application fee (explained on p. 95).

Follow these four steps with great attention to detail and you are almost there.

➢ **DURING THE INTERVIEW**

Your interview will be held at one of the U.S. embassies in the United Kingdom. The U.S. embassy in London, for instance, is on South Audley Street near Marble Arch tube station. During the interview you will be asked to give the reason/s for travelling to the United States. You must convey to the embassy representative that you going there as a student to study, <u>not that you are just going there to play basketball</u>. This is important. When the interviewer asks what your reason is for travelling to the United States, don't say: "I just want to live in the U.S."

Another important thing to understand it that the F-1 visa is only a temporary visa, so you must show strong intent to return to the United Kingdom after your full-time college education ends. Most F-1 visa applications are approved, but <u>the most common reason a student or exchange visitor application is denied is because the applicant has not sufficiently proven to the Visa Officer that he will return to his country after completion of study in the United States</u>. This is your responsibility. To help the officer decide, he or she will ask you to demonstrate how you or your family propose to pay for the first year of your studies. Therefore, you should have with you your financial documentation and/or your scholarship letter from the U.S. university you're planning to attend. Examples of such documents include passports demonstrating travel abroad, bank or salary statements, family documents, or student records. Below is a table of documents you should bring to the visa interview:

What to Bring to the interview

Required Forms	Further Documentation
Passport	U.S. College Scholarship Letter
I-20	Financial Documentation
DS-160	SEVIS Payment Receipt

During the interview, feel free to explain why you chose to study at that specific college or university. Do let the interviewer know you are on a basketball scholarship but remember: you are a student-athlete, and "student" comes first.

F-1 VISA INTERVIEW TIPS

1. What you wear is important. Consider the interview a formal event. Don't show up in sweatpants and a hoodie. Wear a business suit or dress.
2. Be specific when answering questions.
3. Bring bank statements or proof of employment.
4. Provide details of your study plans.
5. Tell the truth.
6. Stay calm, be confident and professional.

➢ **AFTER THE INTERVIEW**

At the end of the interview you will hand over your passport to the officer to be processed and have your visa stamp added. You will proceed to the postal station inside the embassy and arrange for your passport to be sent back to you. This will require a small postage fee that you can pay by cash or debit/credit card. To be reunited with your passport you must be at your address at the scheduled time of delivery, and have on hand a photo identification. You will be required to sign for your passport. Processing times can vary, as the release of your passport is at the discretion of the passport agency or embassy, but it usually takes about a week. With this in mind, make sure you start this process as soon as possible. You can't fly without your passport—an important point I once forgot!

If possible, apply for your visa three months before you travel to the U.S. This will give you plenty of time to complete the above steps and have your visa stamped in your passport in good time. If you have any questions about the process you should can review important information about Admissions/Entry on the Homeland Security Web site.

VISA FEES: REACHING FOR YOUR WALLET, AGAIN

SEVIS Fee ($200)

There is a U.S. $200 (£130) fee called a SEVIS fee. It covers the cost of the computer system used to record your stay in the

United States. This fee is unavoidable. The SEVIS fee must be paid at least three days before the date on your visa interview.

Visa Application Fee ($160)

You will also need to pay an additional $160 (£110) for the visa application fee in the United Kingdom at the U.S. Embassy. Information on where to pay the visa application can be found at the U.S. Embassy website.

Entering the U.S. on a F1-student visa

You've jumped through hoops of fire to get your student visa and now you're all checked in and boarding your flight to the United States. Yet, you still need to make it through customs on the other side. Customs, or Custom and Border Protection (CBP) is an agency of the U.S. government that controls the U.S. border, including airline flights that transport passengers arriving from foreign countries. The customs service has three major missions: collecting tariff revenue, protecting the U.S. economy from smuggled and illegal goods, and processing people and goods at ports of entry. This last part is the reason you will meet briefly with a customs agent immediately after you touch down in the U.S.

While you are in the air on your way to the U.S., the flight attendant will give you an I-94 form. You will fill out this document and give it to the CBP officials when you land. This form will document your authorized stay and is the official record of your permission to be in the U.S. It will be stamped and stapled into your passport. That being said, as of May 25, 2013 the CBP has implemented a new electronic I-94 process so you may not receive a hard copy of the form at all. When dealing with the CBP officials, speak to the point and answer only the questions you're asked, don't offer any extra information. This can lead to further questions and delays—long delays.

Re-entering the United States

However excited you are to leave home and live a life of independence, you will probably want to return to the U.K. once or twice to see family and friends during your four-year stay. To depart from the U.S. and ensure a smooth reentry, there are important tasks you must remember to complete before leaving.

Most importantly, you must speak with your international student advisor, or what Homeland Security calls the **Designated School Official (DSO)**. Every college has a DSO who generally works in the school's international student office. You must have a current SEVIS Form I-20 endorsed for travel and your DSO needs to be able to verify that your SEVIS record is accurate and up-to-date. <u>Whatever your do, don't board a flight leaving the U.S. without speaking with your DSO.</u>

FIVE VISA FAQs

1. **What if I have an expired passport or one that will expire in less than six months?**

You must renew your passport before entering or reentering the United States. In most cases, to enter the U.S. you must have a passport that is valid for at least six months after the date you enter or reenter.

2. How long can I stay in the U.S. with an F-1 visa?

When you enter the U.S., an immigration officer at the port of entry will issue you an I-94 card that indicates your non-immigrant status (F1) and your authorized stay. It is typically "Duration of Status" or "D/S" on a student's I-94 card, meaning that you may remain in the U.S. as long as you are enrolled in the school to complete your academic program. After the program ends you will have 60 days to depart the U.S.

3. What if my F-1 student visa has expired?

You can stay in the United States on an expired F-1 visa as long as you maintain your student status. However, if you are returning home or traveling to a country where automatic revalidation does not apply, you must have a valid visa to return to the United States.

4. Can I transfer to a different college while I'm in the U.S.?

Yes. You must notify your current school and work with the designated school official (DSO) to transfer your SEVIS record. You also need to obtain a new I-20 from your new school, and give the completed I-20 to your new DSO within 15 days of transfer date.

5. I couldn't think of a fifth question, but the title "Four VISA FAQs" sounded silly. Anyhow, here's one more important point:

Never make final travel plans until you have your visa approved. Attaining your F-1 visa is a relatively simple process. However, keep in mind that visa issuance is not guaranteed. If your visa is denied, you will be given a reason based on the section of law which applies to your ineligibility. Filing a waiver of ineligibility is possible in some cases. [1]

6

NCAA Eligibility: Staying Inside the Red Tape

STAYING ELIGIBLE

I once prayed to God for a bike, but quickly found out he didn't work that way...so I stole a bike and prayed for his forgiveness.

—ANONYMOUS

I asked a ref if he could give me a technical foul for thinking bad things about him. He said, of course not. I said, "Well, I think you stink." And he gave me a technical. You can't trust 'em.

—JIM VALVANO

So far, we've talked about how to gain exposure, how to apply to college, and how to secure your visa. Now we want to make sure you efforts aren't in vain. Although it is not a government entity, the National Collegiate Athletics Association (NCAA) is the governing body of collegiate athletics in the United States and Canada. The NCAA writes the rules for competition, including eligibility rulings. To become eligible to play college basketball you must meet certain requirements. Could LeBron James go back and play college ball if he wanted? No: he's too old, has played professional basketball, and wouldn't be eligible. Eligibility requirements are put in place to ensure fair competition. You must consider the NCAA rulings very carefully when creating your strategy for getting a scholarship offer, as penalties for rule violations can be harsh and include bans from playing basketball for up to a year—and in some cases, forever.

To be cleared to compete in the NCAA, you first need to register with the **NCAA Initial Eligibility Center**. Any college-bound student-athlete (incoming freshman or first-year enrollee) interested in enrolling at an NCAA Division I or II college or university—and competing as a varsity student-athlete on behalf of that NCAA school's intercollegiate athletics program—must receive an academic and amateurism evaluation certification decision from the NCAA Eligibility Center. British student-athletes should register with the Initial Eligibility Clearinghouse no later than October during their second year of sixth-form to be eligible for competition the following academic year. The U.S. college academic year typically begins in August so you will register 10 months prior to starting college. It's incumbent on the student-athlete to collect and submit all the required information to the Initial Eligibility Center. The NCAA will take it from there. If you're confused or have questions, pick up the phone and call the school's NCAA **compliance officer** who will guide you through the process.

**Note: The NCAA's Golden Rule: A student-athlete shall complete his or her seasons of participation within five calendar years from the beginning of the athletes first college semester. In other words, the NCAA gives you five years to play four (in case you get injured, transfer colleges, etc.)

There are two basic requirements that you must fulfil in order to play:

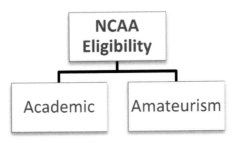

1. ACADEMIC ELIGIBILITY

Your eligibility will be determined—in part—by your education, such as schools you have attended and your qualifications (GCSEs and A-levels). The educational system in the U.S. is very different from the U.K. and there are a few things you need to know to make the transition go smoothly. To participate in Division I or Division II athletics, or to receive an athletics scholarship during the first year of college, a student athlete must:

➤ Graduate from high school

➤ Complete a minimum of 16 core courses

➤ Earn a minimum required grade-point average in core courses

➤ Earn a qualifying test score on either the SAT or the ACT[i]

---

[i] The ACT is an achievement test containing up to 5 components: English, Mathematics, Reading, Science, and an optional Writing Test. Some schools require the ACT, others do not.

➢ Request final amateurism certification from the NCAA Eligibility Center.

For Division I student-athletes who will enroll August 1, 2016 and later, the requirements to compete in the first year will change. In addition to the above standards, students must:

➢ Earn at least a 2.3 (out of a 4.0) grade-point average in core courses.

➢ Meet an increased sliding-scale standard (for example, an SAT score of 820 requires a 2.5 high school core course GPA, while a lower SAT score requires a higher GPA).

➢ Successfully complete 10 of the 16 total required core courses before the start of their seventh semester in high school. Seven of the 10 courses must be successfully completed in English, Math and Science.

Bear in mind that these requirements are based on the U.S. education system. It's your job to have your school translate your qualifications (GCSEs and A-Levels) into equivalent grades before sending them to the NCAA Initial Eligibility Center.

**Important: *NCAA Division III colleges and universities set their own admission standards. The NCAA does not set initial eligibility requirements in Division III.*

Once prospective student-athletes are cleared to compete, they must continue to meet academic and amateurism benchmarks to stay eligible. These often are referred to as "continuing-eligibility" or "progress-toward-degree" rules. The purpose of these rules is for all student-athletes to be continually on track to earn their diplomas. In order to remain eligible during your first year of college, you must earn at least nine credits[ii] during the first term.

If a student-athlete earns at least nine credits in the first term, he or she can continue to practice the remainder of the year. If not, he or she can remain on aid but can't practice.

This is a lot of information to take in, I know. At the end of the day, if you are on top of your academics in the U.K., meeting these requirements should not be an issue. A few U.K. basketball players *have* had eligibility issues in the past, but most are not due to poor academic performance. The players who run into trouble with their eligibility are typically caught by the NCAA's lesser-known rules. This happened to Tom Ward, English-born in 1988. Ward travelled to the U.S. to play high school ball after completing his GCSEs, only to find himself ineligible to play.

TOM WARD'S STORY

Ward played his youth basketball for the Sussex-based Brighton Bears Juniors. He was always an intensely-motivated player with an insatiable work ethic. I played for the same team as Ward growing up. We went to different secondary schools but spent every weekend and several nights during the week getting up shots in an empty gym or playing pickup games on the Brighton Beach court. Once we had exhausted ourselves on the court, we

---

[ii] A course credit is a unit that gives weighting to the value, level or time requirements of an academic course taken at a school or other educational institution.

would head home to watch VHS tapes of NBA games and play NBA Live on the PS1. We were obsessed with the game and consumed by the desire to get better — to eventually be the best.

By age 17, Ward was one of the top guards in the country and he wanted to take his game to the next level. Over the years, he had watched players at his club make the transition to the U.S. His former teammate, Richard Midgely, had journeyed to the States a few years earlier to play for a high school called Modesto Christian in California before earning a full basketball scholarship at the University of California at Berkeley. So Ward reached out to Midgley for help. Midgely put Ward in contact with a guy named Randy Anderson who was affiliated with Midgely's high school as well as the local church. Anderson agreed to help Ward come to the U.S. to study at Modesto and play on its basketball team. He reached out to families that might like to host Ward during his studies. After only a brief search, Anderson found the Puthuff family who said they would be delighted to be Ward's host family and agreed to let Ward live with the family in their California home. Once his accommodation and enrollment were finalized, all Ward had to do was apply for his F1-student visa. Everything was going to plan. Ward made the trip overseas to his temporary home in California.

It was only after he arrived in California and settled in that Ward got the news that he was ineligible for the upcoming season. Because Ward had completed his GCSEs in England, he was already considered graduated by the California state education system. According to the NCAA, student-athletes have graduated from high school after completing GCSEs/Standard Grades (typically age 16). Once graduated, student-athletes have the option of playing a year basketball during a **postgraduate year** at a prep school before they enroll at a U.S. college or university. This applies to NCAA division I and II. Tom's year at Modesto Christian would not be considered a postgraduate year because this school did not offer this interim year (somewhat like a Gap Year in the UK). Tom would be allowed to study and practice with the team as well as take advantage of the U.S. Amateur Athletic Union (AAU) circuit in the summer to gain exposure, but he would never play a single game for Modesto Christian High School.

This was an obvious disappointment for Ward. If he had known about these eligibility rulings earlier this situation may have been avoided, or Ward could have looked for another high school. There are a couple of ways Ward could have avoided—and you can avoid—these infringements. One option is to not sit your GCSE examinations—but this is not a good idea. Even if you live and breathe the game and it seems like basketball is your "be-all and end-all," your education still comes first. Basketball will consume only a small portion of your life while a good education will pay dividends forever. Another option is to sit your GCSE examinations and As & A2 examinations and then find a U.S. high school that offers a postgraduate year.

If you choose to spend a year at a U.S. high school before progressing to a 4-year college, ideally, you would complete your GCSEs and A2 levels in the U.K. before transferring to a high school that offers a year of postgraduate study. Now, here is another warning: attending a **prep school** for longer than one year will effectively delay enrollment and lead to punishment from the NCAA. For example, if you complete your GCSEs/Standard Grades and move to the States for two years of high school before enrolling in college, you will be ineligible for the first year of college. This first year, during which you must sit out is called a **year-in-residence**. You can attend classes and practice with the team but you can't play in games. After this you will have only three years of eligibility remaining. If you attend high and/or prep school for three years, you will be required to sit out your first year of college (year in residence) and will have only two years of eligibility remaining. Not only will this limit college playing time; it may make it harder for you to get offered a scholarship. College coaches prefer to recruit players who have four years of eligibility remaining so they have time for player development.

Ward was not the only U.K. player to run into issues with eligibility. Unfortunately, other British players have had to learn the eligibility rules the hard way.

ORLAN JACKMAN'S STORY

Orlan Jackman is a guy who knows the ins and outs of U.S. college basketball more than most. London-born Jackman got his U.S. breakthrough in 2006 shortly after returning from a European Championship in Romania where he competed for Great Britain U21s. A 6'5" forward with natural athleticism, a tenacious work ethic and skills to match, Jackman was a coach's delight. A coach in Romania, after being impressed with Jackman's play during the tournament, referred him to Army & Navy Academy, a high school in Carlsbad, California, where he could develop his skills, play competitive basketball and hopefully get recruited by a Division I college. Jackman enrolled at Army & Navy and played for the school during the 2006-2007 season.

Despite a successful high school senior year, Jackman was not heavily recruited by college coaches. Yet his recruiting woes weren't due to his poor play on the court. California state rules that govern education and athletics caused Jackman to be a red flag in his recruiting class: California has its own rules that say that if you haven't lived in the U.S. for at least one year, you can't get a scholarship at a California junior college straight from high school.

Jackman became un-recruitable by many college coaches, and without an obvious next step in the U.S., Jackman was forced to return to England. But despite the setback he did not give up on his dream of playing college ball. Jackman had made such an impression during his short time in the U.S. that he was still being actively recruited by college coaches even while back in the U.K. Jackman remembers this time fondly: "Being wanted is an incredible feeling." And one of these colleges that wanted him was Seminole State College.

Seminole State is a public **junior college** in Oklahoma. Oklahoma is located slap bang in the middle of the United States, a region of the country that's flat, sparse and pretty much devoid of anything. But this is where Jackman found his new home. For athletes who have dreams of playing college basketball, junior college can be a stepping-stone between high school and a four-year college. It is an all-around opportunity to get better—to refine your skills on the court while improving your grades in the classroom. A lot of major college coaches recruit heavily from junior colleges. Marquette University head coach Buzz Williams is one of them: "Anytime there's a delay in someone's dream, their hunger and their fight to accomplish their dream is heightened."[1] This is what can make junior college recruits so appealing. Jackman played at Seminole State for two years before accepting a scholarship at NCAA Division II Newman University in Kansas. At the time, Jackman thought he would be able to use all three of his remaining years of eligibility at Newman, and was confident that this would be his final college destination.

The NCAA: A Little Give-and-Take

As you can tell, the NCAA guidelines governing education and eligibility are very rigid. However, there is a little bit of leeway for athletes who have just completed their GCSEs to save their eligibility. The NCAA recognizes that in Britain, prospective student-athletes can continue studying at a British secondary school for further qualifications (As & A2's) which are necessary for qualification for British Universities. The NCAA will move back the graduation date for the following qualifications: For As and the BTEC National Certificate, graduation is moved back **1 year**. For A-Level, graduation is moved back **2 years** (both require two or more exams passed with grades of E or higher). For Scottish Highers, the BTEC National Diploma, and NVQ level 3, graduation is moved back **two years**. This means that although you are considered graduated, after you have completed your GCSEs, the NCAA will allow you to study for a further two years towards your A-levels without using up any of your college eligibility.

An important point to note: The NCAA does not recognize equivalencies to AS levels in accordance with the UCAS system — prospective players must complete the full two-year course.[2]

➤ AS, BTEC National Certificate + 1 year = eligible to play free of punishment.

➤ A-level Scottish Highers + 1 year = eligible to play free of punishment.

➤ BTEC Dip, NVQ level 3 + 1 year = eligible to play free of punishment.

2. AMATEURISM

According the NCAA, amateurism rules ensure that students' number-one priority is to obtain a quality education — AND that all student-athletes compete equitably. All incoming student-athletes must be certified as amateurs. With global recruiting becoming more common, determining the amateur status of prospective student athletes can be challenging. All student-athletes, including international students, are required to adhere to NCAA amateurism requirements to remain eligible for intercollegiate competition. And these rules don't apply just while you are *in* college. The NCAA will look back at your playing history to make sure you have never violated any of the following rules.

In general, amateurism requirements <u>do not allow</u>:

- Contracts with professional teams
- Salary for participating in athletics
- Prize money above actual and necessary expenses
- Playing with professionals
- Tryouts, practice or competition with professional teams
- Receiving benefits from an agent or prospective agent
- Agreeing to be represented by an agent
- Delaying initial full-time collegiate enrollment to participate in organized sports competition

Jackman's tangle with the NCAA continues

Unfortunately for Jackman, his trouble with the NCAA was not over. This time it was over amateurism. After a great preseason at Newman, and just four hours before Newman was to play in an exhibition game against number-three-ranked Kansas State, Jackman was informed he was ineligible for the coming season and would have to sit out. This was a huge blow.

The issue was that Jackman had played club basketball while back in the U.K.—without attending any educational institution. During the 2005-2006 season, Jackman played for Hackney White Heat, and according to the NCAA, this used one year of eligibility. During 2006-2007 he played for Army & Navy High School in the U.S. (using his second year). During 2007-2008 he played for Manchester Magic (his third). His last season at Seminole State used up his fourth year. (He was actually at Seminole State for two years but during his last season he got a medical **redshirt**[iii] after breaking his foot in the second game of the season). Under NCAA rules, Jackman was considered graduated as soon as he left his school in the U.K. From this moment, ANY organized basketball he played counted against his four years of college eligibility.

Where others would have called it a day and jumped on the next flight to sunny old England, Jackman saw this as just another obstacle he had to conquer. Jackman possesses a quality that is vital for success: the ability to cope with setbacks, apparent failure or disappointment, and to use what he learns to move forward. Jackman began seeking other options and opportunities to keep playing the game he loved. That's when Jackman heard about NAIA schools. NAIA stands for (the) National Association of Intercollegiate Athletics and is the governing body for many four-year schools that are simply not NCAA members. Although NAIA schools typically attract less-talented athletes than NCAA schools, the NAIA still comprises a collection of highly-competitive athletics programs. Jackman found that the NAIA clearinghouse was a lot less stringent than the NCAA clearinghouse and would allow him to regain his playing eligibility. He finished his career at Oklahoma City University, averaging 11.7 points and 5.5 rebounds per game and is now playing professional basketball in Europe.

[iii] **redshirt** is a delay or suspension of an athlete's participation in order to lengthen his or her period of eligibility

PRO BASKETBALL: MAINTAINING AMATEUR STATUS

Let's take a deeper dive into NCAA amateurism. As we know, a potential student-athlete needs to meet certain criteria in order to be eligible for competition. The NCAA will look to see if you still qualify as an amateur and not a professional.

The NCAA identifies a professional team as one from which any of its players receive more than actual and necessary expenses for participation on that team, except as otherwise permitted by the NCAA. Actual and necessary expenses are limited to the following, provided the value of these items is commensurate with the fair market value in the locality of the player(s) and is not excessive in nature:

1. Meals directly tied to competition and practice held in preparation for such competition
2. Lodging directly tied to competition and practice held in preparation for such competition
3. Apparel, equipment and supplies
4. Coaching and instruction
5. Medical insurance
6. Transportation (expenses to and from practice competition, cost of transportation from home to training/practice site at the beginning of the season and from training/practice site to home at the end of season)
7. Medical treatment and physical therapy.

8. Facility usage

9. Entry fees

10. Other reasonable expenses[3]

Boy, there is a lot to remember. But if you remember only two things, remember these:

1. You are allowed to play basketball on a professional team in the U.K. as long as you <u>do not</u> receive benefits that exceed reasonable expenses.

2. You must play within the time of formal education towards graduation or during the one year after graduation.

Rule 1 means that you will remain eligible as long as you do not receive an income from playing basketball. It means that the club can pay for your jersey and possibly travel expenses, but it cannot pay for anything that doesn't go directly towards basketball.

Rule 2 actually works to your advantage. It means that you can stay in Britain and play basketball for a professional team after your finish your A2's as long as you are still not getting paid. You will not jeopardize your eligibility and it will give you time to find the right college in the U.S. This rule helped Tom Ward extend his search for a college in the U.S. while continuing to play ball. Here's how:

Ward finally gets a U.S. college scholarship

After sitting his senior year at Modesto Christian in California, and without any college scholarship offers, Ward returned to Europe to play basketball in Gran Canarias, Spain, while attending the Canarias Basketball Academy (CBA). CBA is a private academic institution that offers a college preparatory education as well as coaching to improve basketball skills. At CBA, Ward concentrated on improving his game while buying some time to be picked up by a college recruiter. And this is exactly what happened. Rob Orellana, the head coach at CBA, was in constant contact with college recruiters in the U.S. and regularly invited them to his academy in Spain to recruit. Ward impressed a college coach from St. Francis College in Brooklyn, New York, and was offered an official visit, which he accepted. Ward made a good impression on the visit and was offered a scholarship to play for St. Francis in the Northeast Athletic Conference. Ward's circuitous path had finally landed him a D1 scholarship offer. The best things in life don't come easy.

After a year with limited playing time at St. Francis, Ward decided to transfer schools. Under the NCAA regulations, Ward would have to sit out a year if he transferred from one Division I school to another Division I school. However, the NCAA says that you do not have to sit out a year if you transfer from a DI to a DII school. So with an eagerness to play, that's exactly what Ward did. He transferred from DI St. Francis to DII St. Michael's College—in Vermont—and immediately became an impact player.

Enduring the Struggle: Today it's a Choice

Some of history's best mathematicians, scientists, and innovators spend years working on a single problem. They struggled, they hit dead ends, they chased their tails looking for answers, they started over after months of prodding and poking. But the common trait of every man or woman at the top of his or her field is that they endure. Mastering the struggle isn't always easy but a persistent spirit is the key to success. This is what Plato, Einstein and Mozart all had.

But in today's world of instant gratification and constant distraction, it's hard to stay focused on a single goal. Today, we're used to having all our senses stimulated all the time and feel unengaged if they're not. We're all guilty of it. We all browse the Internet on our laptops while watching television or listen to music while we're supposed to be working. Some will claim that they are multitasking; but really, multitasking is a myth. So-called multitaskers are actually *serial tasking*. Rather than engaging in simultaneous tasks they are shifting from one task to another in rapid succession. It is neither effective nor productive. But we have become accustomed to these simultaneous activities in our everyday lives. Our eyes and ears are constantly alert to the information that saturates our environment. People today tend to get bored easily and are quick to go in search of alternative activities. It's sad, but true.[4]

In order to achieve success, we must fight distractions. Today more than ever, it's hard to stay focused and endure the struggle, but it is necessary to achieve success. Little by little, day by day, if you are patient and focused, you will succeed. Endure the struggle.

Transferring Colleges

The NCAA has certain rules to try and limit the amount of transfers. To deter student-athletes from transferring from a DI to a DI, the NCAA requires athletes to sit out a year before they can play. They don't want DIII to become a minor league for college basketball where schools call up players freely when they want to use them.

The reason there's no penalty for transferring to a DIII school is this: There are no scholarships at DIII so A) the DI school gets its scholarship money back, and B) the DIII school gets a player that can be valuable to its program at no cost (and the student athlete will most likely get more playing time). Everybody wins.

You must make sure you abide to these rules years before attending college to remain eligible. As always, make sure you know this stuff and plan ahead.

TOOLS & TRICKS

NCAA Resources

- ➢ **NCAA Eligibility Center:**
  http://web1.ncaa.org/ECWR2/NCAA_EMS/NCAA.jsp

- ➢ **Division I Eligibility Toolkit:** www.ncaa.org/student-athletes/resources/division-i-initial-eligibility-toolkit

- ➢ **FAQs for International College-Bound Student-Athletes:**
  http://fs.ncaa.org/Docs/eligibility_center/Student_Resources/International_Student_FAQ.pdf

➢ **Initial Eligibility Center: International Student Frequently Asked Questions:**
http://grfx.cstv.com/photos/schools/beth/genrel/auto_pdf/InternationalStudentsFAQ.pdf

❼

Welcome to U.S. College Life

LET ME INTRODUCE YOU TO YOUR
NEW FAMILY AND FRIENDS

"You have brains in your head. You have feet in your shoes. You can steer yourself any direction you choose. You're on your own. And you know what you know. And YOU are the one who'll decide where to go..."

—DR. SEUSS, OH, THE PLACES YOU'LL GO!

Most international students studying in the U.S. are assigned a **host family** by the college. Host families help foreign students feel welcome and assist them as they settle into their new lives in the Unites States. Both the student and the host family are enriched by the friendships and cultural exchanges during their time spent in the host family program. Students are encouraged to connect with their host families prior to their arrival in the U.S. so they can get to know one another and possibly arrange a ride from the airport to the college campus. I did all of the above before I arrived at Charlotte-airport near Davidson College. I was assigned the Gruber family and met Chris (host dad), Tim (host brother) and Greta Gruber (host sister) at the airport. The next morning I was introduced to host mum Dana Gruber, who said she would be taking me up to the college campus the next morning to move in to my college dorm room. The entire Gruber family were so kind to me, but none more so than host mum, Dana.

Dana made sure I felt at home in the U.S. So, without request, Dana decided to be my tea supplier during college. My preferred brand of English tea was hard to come by and couldn't be found anywhere near the college campus. Therefore, Dana took it upon herself to bring a new shipment of tea to my dorm room every week. She was giving me enough tea to quench the thirst of the entire campus, but as not to be rude, I accepted each delivery with gratitude. "This is great, I was almost out," I lied, and began to stockpile the tea in the corner of my dorm room. My stash would grow so large that by the end of the year I could have probably recreated the 1773 Boston Tea Party!

ARRIVING ON CAMPUS

I arrived on campus for the first time to sub-tropical heat and blistering sunshine. The cold weather clothes that I had been wearing in London the day before were now sticking to my skin with sweat, so I changed out of my jeans and headed to the **student union** for registration. As soon as I got there I was approached by a guy, probably an older student, wearing sandals, a grass skirt and multicolored Hawaiian leis stacked around his neck. He took one off, placed it around my neck and swiveled me around to face a guy with a camera who took my picture. I was then shoveled inside the student union. It was chaos inside with parents and family members saying last minute goodbyes so I quickly checked myself in and headed to the basketball area to meet the coaching staff.

Dana then took me over to my dormitory. It's normal for college freshmen to live in one small room— with a roommate. I found my room and opened the door. The room was filled with people. I stood there a moment before my new roommate stepped forward out of the crowd and introduced himself. The other people in the room were his family members, including his parents, brother, aunt and grandmother. He had already unpacked a lot of his stuff and it looked as though he'd brought everything he owned. But, there I was, fresh off my transatlantic flight, with one suitcase weighing no more than 50kg and a considerable-sized piece of hand luggage. The next thing that caught my eye were the beds—bunked beds. I thought I'd left these days behind me, but in the U.S. bunked beds and freshman year go hand-in-hand. It's ironic, really. College is supposed to mark the beginning of adulthood and maturity but shortly after you wave goodbye to your parents and a life of dependence, you jump back into a kiddy bunk bed. For at least the first year of college you will sleep in the same bed as another adult of the same sex… just try not to think of it that way.

IN THE WORDS OF ALLEN IVERSON:
"YOU TALKIN' 'BOUT PRACTICE?"[i]

"Ben, we have Red Rack at 5" shouted an upperclassman as I started walking from the basketball locker room towards the college cafeteria.

"What's Red Rack?" I said.

"Just be outside the back of the arena at 5, by the loading dock. And make sure all of the other freshmen are there too!"

"Red Rack?" I thought to myself, puzzled. Is it a type of workout? Do I need to be in my athletic clothes? These were the necessary questions I should have asked but the moment had passed and my teammate was now out of earshot. Most people fear the unexpected but I hate it with a passion. I like to be in control and I feel vulnerable when I walk into situations unprepared. The nervousness seeped into my body and I no longer had the appetite for the cafeteria. Alone, I walked back to my freshman dorm to search for one of my classmates in the hope that he would be able to fill me in.

Fortunately one of the other freshman basketball players and my fellow classmate, Brendan McKillop, was the coach's son. Brendan had been around Davidson basketball since the day his young and delicate eardrums could endure 7,000 roaring Davidson basketball fans inside Belk Arena. His father has been the head

---

[i] If you've not seen Allen Iverson's interview about practice, here it is: www.youtube.com/watch?v=eGDBR2L5kzl

coach at Davidson since the day he was born and their house was a stone's throw away from campus.

"It's hard to explain," said Brendan. "It's basically a box..." he paused. "No, more of a 3-D rectangle made out of metal scaffolding and stood on its end. It's about nine feet high. And it's painted red. That's why they call it Red Rack."

"Ok. But what's it for?" I pushed for the more important information. I wanted to know what exactly the red rack had to do with me. "Chin-ups and dips," Brendan began to explain. It sounded like an elaborate playground apparatus that you might find at the park. And it was just that.

How it worked was that you partnered up with a teammate and find some space on the red rack. You then have to reach up and grab a horizontal piece of scaffold. When the coaches start the timer, you pull yourself off the ground and start doing chin-ups. You have completed a full chin-up only when you've managed to pull your body up and hook your chin over the bar. You must then let yourself drop back down so you're hanging from the bar with your arm straight before starting the next chin-up. The goal is to do as many chin-ups as you can in one minute. If your arms fatigue and you can't do another complete chin up, your partner will assist you by lifting your legs so that you are high enough to hook your chin over the bar. Then you have to support your body weight in that position until the minute is up. Once you're done, your partner goes.

After you and your partner have done a minute of chin-ups, you do the same again for 45 seconds.

The Red Rack also has short horizontal struts that poke out; these are used for dips[ii]. Using the same principle, you and your partner complete a minute, then 45 seconds of dips. Red Rack is always on a Friday after a long week of workouts and your arms fatigue quickly. There's always a noticeable difference between how many chin-ups and dips the seniors can manage compared to the underclassmen. Three years of practice and greater physical maturity prevented any of the freshmen from showing up their older classmates.

The player has a love-hate relationship with the Red Rack. It is a grueling few minutes that takes hold of your day as you find yourself sitting in class thinking about Red Rack—and a feeling of dread begins squeezing your stomach. But on the brighter side, Red Rack also marks the end of the week and leads into a day of rest.

How to Push Through Fatigue: Pain Signaling vs. Pain Perception

Why do we stop running? Why do we hunch over with our hands on our knees and gasp for breath? Why do we give up altogether? We usually say it's because we're hurt or tired. This is what people say before they decide it's time to go home. But most of the time we just use these

---

[ii] The dip is an exercise used in strength training. Narrow, shoulder-width dips primarily train the triceps.

excuses to bail ourselves out of something we no longer want to do. Could we train harder, run farther or jump higher if we tried? The answer is yes. This is because we usually surrender to our emotions more quickly than we surrender to physical pain. **Pain signaling** is fairly simple. It's a biological process brought about by chemical responses in your body to stimuli around you. There are pain neurons throughout the body called nociceptors that send out pain signals whenever they sense bodily harm. Once activated, they shoot chemical signals along your spine to your brain. The signals enter your awareness and you say "ouch." This is the scientific version of pain.

The not-so-scientific, more psychological version of pain is **pain perception**. While the signaling of pain is pretty straightforward, the perception of pain is much more fluid and abstract. Sometimes, the nociceptors will send out a tiny spark and you will whimper like a scared puppy. Othertimes your body tells you that you should be writhing in pain but you can hardly feel a thing. This is the result of pain perception. How you perceive pain is controlled exclusively by the brain, which decides how to interoperate the signals sent from different parts of the body, including the receptors in the skin but also the visual information coming in through your eyes.

Have you ever gone "ouch" before you felt any pain and then realized that whatever it was didn't actually hurt? Herein lies the difference between actual pain and the perception of pain. Our pain perception is negative in nearly all cases—there are few who welcome pain with a smile. Most of us perceive pain as suffering, automatically imbuing it with negative emotions. But the silver lining is that it's the psychological or emotional part of pain that can be most easily changed.

We cannot (without medication) change our body's chemical responses but we can change how we perceive things. We just have to coach our own minds. Think about this the next time you're being put through a workout and your legs feel like jelly, your lungs are burning and your stomach is queasy. These are no longer the signs of your own physical suffering. They are the signs that you're getting better—signs that tell you you're a little closer to your final destination. When your coach pushes you during practice he is not only trying to improve your physical skills; he is also working on your mental toughness. He's pushing you to your limits to see how long it takes for you to surrender. Then, hopefully, next time you'll be able to endure a little more. There's a reason behind your pain, and the greater your desire to reach your goal, the more pain you'll be willing to withstand.

Get Comfortable Being Uncomfortable

But how do you develop competitive toughness and the ability to live in the moment? With practice, of course. My coach loved it when we got pissed off after someone scored on us. An apathetic ball player will be a failing ball player. The best way to get tougher is to continually involve yourself in situations where you are challenged. Challenge your friends to play 1-on-1. Never turn down a pickup game. When you do these and other challenging activities, your levels of perseverance and determination get tested. The hope is that these traits become stronger over time. Ever heard of "the survival of the fittest?" This is a phrase originating in the Evolutionary Theory, a perspective in the field of psychology. It was the Evolutionary Psychologist Charles Darwin who said that "during the battle for life, of varieties which possess any advantage in structure, constitution, or instinct, I have called Natural Selection." What he meant by this is that animals (and people) who are best-equipped for life in a particular environment will be the ones who survive, breed, and pass along their genes to the next generation.

Your environment is the basketball court.

The other thing competition teaches you is how to cope with defeat. No matter how good an athlete becomes there will always be a time when they "fail." It is what you do after failure, how you cope, that will determine future outcomes. Basketball is a game of mistakes, missed shots, turnovers and fouls. It happens to everyone, but not everyone responds in the same way. Some people hang their heads and some simply move onto the next play.

You can work on your competitive toughness by playing basketball against the talent in England, but the best way to gauge your ability, compared to players in the United States, is to make the trip across the pond.

TAKING SPACE: IT'S ALL ABOUT REAL ESTATE

Weight, muscle mass and strength are a lot more important in the U.S. game than in Europe. Generally, European players are more slender, traits that lend themselves to a more pass-oriented game of teamwork, fundamentals and finesse. In the U.S. it's more about brute strength, athleticism, and power. In order to get big and strong, you have to work out, and assuredly, just like your mother told you, you have to "eat up."

America is a nation obsessed with food. Stateside, food occupies a great deal of waking thought: the recipes, the snacks, the supermarkets, the cooking shows, the Pinterest boards[iii]. And because people are constantly thinking about food, a bowl of snacks is rarely out of reach. Not only is food always around you; the obsession is more about quantity rather than quality. You know what they say: "Everything is bigger in the USA."

Forget your dainty European portions and forget your meat and two veg. We're talking meat, two veg, extra meat, a couple of starches, a sweet tea and dessert. While the English are balancing delicately-cut, bite-sized pieces of their meal onto the back of their forks, their American counterparts are grabbing at sustenance with their hands. Think about it. Most "All-American food" doesn't require a knife and fork, e.g., cheeseburgers, pizza, French fries. So what does this mean? U.S. food culture is generally bad news for people with the 'fat gene' that's linked to high cholesterol levels and type 2 diabetes but good news for competitive athletes who need to keep their bodies fueled. Food in the U.S. is abundant, calorific and heartily portioned. I was 6'8" and 198½ lb when I arrived at Davidson College. As a forward I was very underweight compared to my teammates and competitors, and during my freshman year I struggled to hold my own on the court. One day we were doing a basketball drill and I was on defense in the post. I had to play defense for a minute straight while my teammates tried to score on me, one after another. I got scored on time after time. My inferior

---

[iii] Pinterest is a pinboard-style photo-sharing Web site that allows users to create and manage theme-based image collections such as events, interests, and hobbies.

physical strength left me unable to defend the rim. I would try and body up on my teammates to create a wall between them and the basket. But they would just hunch down and take a few crab dribbles, bumping me closer and closer to the rim, before making a quick move over either shoulder to score. They started calling me "seafood." I don't know why, but I was as helpless as a shrimp being scooped up in a big trawl net. Or maybe it was because I was about as strong as a shrimp. Either way, it got me all fired up. To further fuel my rage my coach would tell me half-jokingly that I needed to "eat an elephant." I was on the "eat as much as you want of whatever you want" diet. After a lot of weight-lifting and a lot of eating, by the start of my sophomore year, I was up to 235lb. Then, I was the one enjoying a shrimp cocktail. After increasing my weight and strength, I was able to hold my own on the court.

According to the Calumet College of St. Joseph, based on 90 minutes of play, a male basketball player should eat at least 23 calories for each pound of body weight, every day. Female basketball players require between 20 and 23 calories per pound daily.[1] At 6'9" and weighing around 235lb during college, according to the Calumet study, I had to eat 5,405 calories a day to maintain my weight. Keep in mind that the recommended daily allowance for an average male is approximately 2,000 calories per day. I would have to eat more than double that to refuel my body and maintain weight after daily workouts. But this is still nothing compared to what some athletes eat on a daily basis. Take Michael Phelps, for instance. You might start to feel malnourished when you hear what he eats for breakfast: three fried egg sandwiches with cheese, lettuce, tomatoes, fried onions, and mayo, one five-egg omelets, a bowl of grits (porridge-like breakfast food made from corn), three slices of French toast with powdered sugar, three chocolate chip pancakes, and two cups of coffee. Phelps consumes 12,000 calories a day while in training. Being able to swallow this amount of food alone requires practice. But America is the best place in the world to train.[2]

Survival of Fittest: An Evolutionary Perspective

It isn't where you came from, it's where you're going that counts.

—ELLA FITZGERALD

Exposure is the condition of "being presented to view" or "made known." Basketball players looking for college scholarships need exposure. They need to put their talents on display in front of scouts and college recruiters. I grew up in a small village called Partridge Green in southeast England. It's a quaint farming village with only a small primary school, butchers, bakers, a farm shop and a doctor's office as the main conveniences. The village is surrounded by green fields and the nearest town is a 20-minute drive away. The village is more of a breeding ground for cows and sheep than talented basketball players, and it comes as no surprise that I am the only U.S. college basketball player that Partridge Green has ever produced. To play organized basketball I had to make a 40-minute drive to the nearest town, Hayward's Heath. I did this once a week, participating in back-to-back training sessions. The boys in the first session were generally my age; the boys in the second were in my brother's age group—he was two school years ahead of me. I also played for a National League team,

Brighton Bears Juniors. This team practiced on Sundays and my mum had to make another 40-minute trip, this time in the opposite direction. All in all, I had two practices a week, each for about two hours.

Outside of those practices, I would take my basketball to school with me and play by myself during breaks and in my back garden when I got home. Unlike most of my friends, I went to secondary school outside my catchment area because my mum thought I would get a better education—something that was worth the extra travel. She was right: I did get a better education but it made it hard for me to spend time with my friends outside of school. On a rare occasion, one of my friends might come and shoot hoops with me in my back garden. The rest of the time I would spend playing by myself. I even bought one of those 'hoop chutes' that you attach the bottom of the basket and returns to the ball back to you after a made shot. After the hoop my dad constructed from the telegraph pole eventually rotted away and became unusable, my mum decided to have a small basketball court put in our back garden. Our house was built in the middle of an acre of land so there was plenty extra space. My mum hired workmen to lay a concrete surface in the far corner of our back garden and have a hoop erected. When at home, I would spend more time on the court than in the house. But still, I didn't really get a lot of opportunities to really compete in live action against other players. I know I would have been an even better player had I competed more as kid.

Competition is a critical driver for performance on the court. It teaches you several important skills you need to become an exemplary basketball player. Bob McKillop always used the term "**competitive toughness.**" At first, I had no idea what it meant. But after four years of college, and not a day on the court passed by without hearing the phrase, I began to understand the lesson he was trying to teach.

DEFINITION: COMPETITIVE TOUGHNESS

1. LIVE IN THE MOMENT

If you live in the moment you are totally focused on the "now." You have little or no consideration for the past or for the future. You're not thinking of the last play when you missed a shot or how you are going to recover form a 12-point deficit. You are mindful only of the action you are currently taking, whether it's grabbing a rebound or diving for a loose ball. When you live in the moment your mind is not preoccupied with thoughts about saving your energy because you still have a quarter left in the game, or missing a shot because someone once told you you're not good enough. When you live in the moment you don't prioritize because you have only one objective in mind. Living in the moment this way allows you to be free of consequences. And when your actions on the court don't have consequences, you become relaxed and let your instincts take control. It's a mindset. It's a talent you have to practice to develop.

2. MAKE EVERY PLAY COUNT

Every coach is looking for the perfect game. To achieve this, they can't have any of their players taking plays off. Coaches need five guys for 40 minutes. The game doesn't need to be decided in the fourth quarter if you make every play count in the first, second and third. Elite basketball players don't take plays off. You have to be mentally tough to play this way.

3. BE THE LAST TO SURRENDER

There are a lot of theories behind "winning," but here's mine: "the one who wins is the one who is last to surrender." This theory can be tested by playing 1-on-1. There is no hiding in a game of 1-on-1 and there's no taking plays off. Your teammates are not there to bail you out. You will see who gets tired first and who shows signs of surrender by letting their opponent go by them to the rim or shoot an uncontested shot. If you have greater "competitive toughness" than your opponent, you will be the last to surrender.

You need all of these traits to have competitive toughness. And you may have noticed, none of them have anything to do with physical strength, athleticism or stamina. They're all mental aspects of the game. The mental part of the game is more important that the physical because the mind controls the body. Remember:

Your mind will give up 100 times before your body ever does.

—UNKNOWN

HOW TO BECOME A STRAIGHT-A STUDENT

Each individual's academic experience depends entirely on the college, the location, the type of school, and what you make of it. As I talk to other English players who have played basketball in the States, we always connect on some shared experiences but are struck by some stark differences. I can describe some of the major similarities among colleges in the U.S. so you can get an idea of what to expect.

Can I transfer my U.K. grades to a college in the U.S?

It depends. It is common for British students to be missing a GCSE social science requirement when applying to U.S. colleges or universities. Student-athletes must make sure they have a social science course as part of their GCSEs. This is not an issue in Scotland where all students are required to study a social science but it can be for students educated in other U.K regions. Your U.K. courses of study are going to come in particularly handy if you attend a liberal arts school. As I explained earlier, liberal arts schools require you to take courses in a wide range of academic departments. You may be able to check off a couple of these requirements using your A-levels, As levels, or even your GCSEs. Ask your college compliance officer or the academic registrar whether any of your U.K. grades will transfer. The British grades are unlikely to count towards your GPA, but you may be able to knock off a course requirement, giving you more freedom to choose some courses you like.

What is a GPA?

You've probably heard of the abbreviation GPA in popular movies but what does it actually stand for and why is it important? GPA stands for Grade Point Average. It's the numerical measurement of a person's academic performance in U.S. schools and universities. GPA assumes a grading scale of A, B, C, D, and F. Each grade is assigned a number of points. An 'A' grade receives 4 points, a B=3, a C=2, a D=1, and an F=0. So, say that during a given semester you took four classes and were given 2 A's, 1 B, and 1 C. You have accumulated 13 grade points for the semester. You then divide the accumulated grade points by the number of classes you took and you have your GPA. (13/4=3.25), so your GPA is 3.25, which is around a B+ average[3].

What is study hall?

Study hall is a period of time, usually around 7-9 p.m., that's set aside for you to do your homework. It usually takes place in the library where you and you teammates will meet. From a coach's perspective, keeping you on track academically might be more important than your performance on the court. At the end of the day if you don't maintain a certain GPA, you're not allowed to play. Simple as that. Study hall keeps you on track with your classes and ensures that you maintain good study habits. It may seem a bit childish but it lets the coaches know you are doing your work outside of class and it gives them peace of mind. Typically, study hall is required only your freshman year. Once you have demonstrated that you can maintain a solid GPA, the coaches will loosen the reins a little. They will still keep an eye on your grades but study hall won't be compulsory.

COST OF STUDENT LIFE IN THE U.S.

Full ride scholarships are structured such that you should be able to live, study and play basketball without spending a penny. You will have your tuition and meals paid for and you will be given athletic clothes and shoes. However, there are a few hidden costs that may not reveal themselves before you show up on campus—so here's a heads-up.

1. Boarding Costs

Although a full scholarship will cover the cost of boarding at college, it will typically only cover the cost of a double/shared room in a dormitory. Singles, or rooms within an apartment tend to cost more and you may be asked to pay the difference. This could be as much as a couple hundred pounds a year.

2. School Books

If you are on full scholarship with the university, your books will be included in your tuition costs. Each semester you will register for classes and, once you have your reading list, you will be able to visit the campus book store and collect the books required for your courses free of charge. At the end of the semester, most students sell their books back to the college, or on a site like Amazon or Ebay. But, as a scholarship athlete, you will be required to return them to your compliance officer. This is so you aren't making money from them, which could be considered a NCAA violation. The money made from selling the books might be considered as income because you didn't pay for your books in the first place and, under NCAA rules, you are not allowed to receive benefits that are over reasonable expenses.

U.S. Taxes: State and Federal

Albert Einstein once said: "The hardest thing in the world to understand is the income tax." So, if one of the most intelligent men that ever lived struggled to get his head around taxes, don't feel bad if you're a little intimidated by the idea. You're not alone. Growing up, all I knew about taxes was that adults and parents hated paying them but coughed up a check once a year when the tax man came knocking.

It comes as a bit of a surprise the first time someone tells you that *you* have to pay them. And it's especially surprising to an Englishman living in the U.S. (who isn't allowed to vote in *any* U.S. election), and given that "taxation without representation" was one primary cause of the American Revolution. But, alas, these are the hypocrisies we have to live with. I guess it's payback time. The first time I had to pay taxes came towards the end of my freshman year. My international advisor at the college told me I had to register for one of three tax sessions that were being held on campus. I registered immediately, and a week or so later I made my way to the sessions along with the forms I was asked to bring: passport, I-20, previous-year tax form (if applicable), etc. We were in a computer lab and each person was seated in front of a terminal. There were about 20 other students in the room, along with the tax expert who was running the session. We logged in to a Web site to complete our forms online. We went through each section step-by-step with the instructor and finished within a couple of hours. Here's the kicker: students on an F-1 student visa must pay BOTH federal and state income taxes.

Every year you are in the States you will have to go through the same tax process: filling out your tax return (Form 1040NR or 1040NR-EZ) to reconcile your tax liability. Because you will be an F-1 visa holder and non-resident alien who has been in the United

States for the full tax year, you have earned income. (Yes, your scholarship counts as income.)

I had to pay around $1,000 (£670) each semester, which isn't fun; but in the grand scale of things it's not too bad. Just remember: you're getting your entire education and housing paid for you for four years. Just be prepared; you will have to pay the tax man. You won't have to pay it in cash but it will go onto your student bill with the college.

There is some good news! Kind of. You will not be required to pay for either Social Security or Medicare taxes under this F-1 status. But then again, you probably didn't know these taxes existed until a second ago.

Maintenance Money

When I say maintenance money, I'm talking about the money you need to live on: money to buy toothpaste, haircuts, Christmas gifts, etc. Maintenance money is extra money you will need to "get by" and is not provided by the scholarship. For most people in the U.S., this money comes from their parents or a summer savings. Most college students work a job during the summer months while they're not at college. Unfortunately, options are limited for international students who want to pile up some extra dollars while in the States. F-1 visas are intended to enable foreign students to study in the U.S.; hence, there are strict work restrictions and you must remain within the restrictions of your F-1 visa at all times. Students with F-1 visas are generally allowed to work on their university campus for up to 20 hours a week, although you can work full-time during the holidays and vacations. Say, for instance, you want to stay and work out at your college during the summer, you would be allowed to work full time at the university during this time. These types of jobs are often called work-study and can be set up with your college.

All these costs we've talked about can really add up. When budgeting for college, you must also remember that colleges and universities in the U.S. are four years, not three years like in the U.K. You're probably reading this book before you go to college, so well done! You're already a step ahead of the game.

EXTRA READING: EMPLOYMENT OPTIONS FOR F-1 VISA HOLDERS

There are four categories of off-campus employment: 1) optional practical training (OPT); 2) curricular practical training (CPT); 3) severe economic hardship; and 4) approved international organizations. Although there are several options available, I haven't heard of any Division I basketball players involved in any of these programs while in season. There just isn't time. I completed a year of OPT (optional practical training) in the U.S. after I graduated, but that's another story.

➢ **Visit the Department of Homeland Security website for more information**: http://www.uscis.gov/working-united-states/students-and-exchange-visitors/students-and-employment

8

Life in the Colonies

SURVIVAL SKILLS: AN ENGLISHMAN ABROAD

It only takes a room full of Americans for the English and
Australians to realize how much we have in common.

—STEPHEN FRY

I am proud to be an American. Because an American can eat
anything on the face of this earth as long as he has two pieces of
bread.

—BILL COSBY

You will arrive at college in the U.S. as an international
student. But unlike some students who are coming from foreign-
speaking parts of the world and with vast cultural differences, your
culture shock will be a trivial as saying "dude" instead of "mate" or
having to drive two hours into the boonies[i] to find a store (shop)

---

[i] The sticks, in the middle of nowhere. Usually associated with living out in the
country.

that carries Wine Gums, Lucozade, or Multesers. You may get homesick from time to time, but as far as the disorientation you might feel when experiencing an unfamiliar way of life, you really won't feel a thing. U.S. and U.K. culture is as close as you are going to get between two countries that are 3,000 miles apart. So don't fret it; your mum can always send a parcel with Curley Wurleys, Chocolate Digestives and PG Tips. But as an Englishman in America, get ready to stand out like a sore thumb.

Being a basketball player, chances are you're pretty tall. If you're an extreme outlier on the height chart, even just in the upper quartile, you probably have to deal with the hassle of people's gawks, ridiculous questions, and awkward hugs. At 6'9" myself, I feel your pain. I live in constant fear that my hearing is going bad. Loud environments aren't comfortable settings for tall people. If I'm in a loud bar, people forget that I don't have ears in my nipples. They speak to my chest and I spend half the time trying to interpret the few sound waves that are funneled up my septum towards my chest. Coupled with the fact that my conversation companion and I usually have extremely different accents—and we'd have trouble understanding each other in the quietest of settings—we usually give up on the conversation pretty quickly and return to awkwardly sipping our drinks. On the brighter side, tall people can walk through crowds like Moses parting the Red Sea. Oh, and we never lose sight of our friends.

AMERICA: A BIRD'S-EYE VIEW

Everything in the U.S. is built for convenience. Buildings are tall and square, cars are boxy and everything just makes sense. As an Englishman living in the U.S., I get asked a lot of questions about life back home: Why do you still have a Queen? Who are those men in tall, furry hats standing outside Buckingham Palace? Why do you hold your fork like that? Over the years of answering the same questions, I lost the energy for lengthy replies. Now, my usual response is, "That's just the way we do things."

But the real reason the British way of life might seem strange to others is that we didn't have the answers when the foundations of the British Empire were laid. Britain today is the result of centuries of guesswork and trial and error, while America's creators had the opportunity to look back in history and draw an outline before starting work. But Brits enjoy upholding our strange traditions, even if they seem backwards or don't make sense. Maypole dancing, cheese rolling, Guy Fawkes night and Morris dancing make Britain Britain.

The physical structure of the U.S. is also different.

If you look at London's roads from a bird's-eye view, it looks like a big tangle of squiggles and knots. On the contrary, if you look at the streets of New York City, they look like a piece of squared paper: grid-like and sensibly named. I say that the Romans built straight roads, the Americans built straight roads, and somewhere in-between Brits must have started drinking.

But as you walk around a new city you'll start to notice landmarks and restaurants that you had only seen in movies and weren't sure if they were real or part of the stage production. I can tell you that Hooters from *Big Daddy (1999)* and Bubba Gump Shrimp from the movie *Forest Gump (1994)* are both fully functioning restaurants. When you get here, check them out.

BUGS AND STUFF: KEEPING THE "OUTDOORS"... OUTDOORS

My mum won't go for a walk over the field in the height of the English summer without wearing a pair of thick jeans, her socks pulled up and a pair of knee-high wellington boots. Don't get me wrong, she's an adventurous, outgoing woman who loves the outdoors; she's just terrified of snakes. When we were kids we used to hide behind doorways in our house and make hissing sounds by passing air through our clenched teeth in an attempt to scare her. Her terror was funny to us. She even used to have nightmares about them, and some mornings my siblings and I would to wake up to screams coming from my mum's room.

My mum used to wake up at 6 am promptly every morning. We had a white cat with black splotches called Inky and my mum was the only person in the family to feed him, which was the first thing she did after she woke. Inky got used to the routine and would make sure he was back in the house by 6 AM after a night of hunting mice, patrolling the village, climbing fences, attending "catnip sniffers anonymous" meetings, and whatever else cats do at night. Inky wasn't known as the most patient cat in the world and instead of waiting in the utility room (where he was fed) for his breakfast he would make his way upstairs to my mum's bedroom. If my mum didn't wake up to his incessant meows, Inky would jump up on her bed. And, if my mum's feet happened to be poking out the bottom of her sheets, Inky would gently bite her toes as a reminder that it was time for breakfast. Now, if my mum was dreaming about snakes the same time Inky bit down (albeit gently) with his pointy cat teeth, my mum would think she was being attacked by snakes and wake up screaming. This happened on a pretty regular basis. God forbid my mum was actually being attacked, because I can assure you we were used to this wakeup call and help was not on the way.

The reason we used to tease my mum so bad is because there is only really two species of snake in England; the adder (the poisonous one) and the grass snake (the only one you're ever likely to see). I lived in England for 16 years and only ever saw two snakes in nature—both non venomous and non-threatening grass snakes. I *did* see a slow worm once, but that's basically a legless lizard. This makes my mum's fear of snakes totally irrational. If she lived in certain parts of the U.S., however, I might be willing to take her anxiety over snakes a little more seriously.

Before I moved to the state of North Carolina in the U.S., I did a little research on the place. My first source, obviously, was Wikipedia. As soon as I started reading, I was reminded of the book, *A Walk in the Woods* by travel writer Bill Bryson. On a whim of stupidity and probably a fair amount of hops, Bryson decided to make it his quest to walk the entire Application Trail. The Appalachian Trail starts in Georgia and runs through North Carolina on its way to New Hampshire and finally Maine. Its total length is approximately 2,200 miles. At the time, walking the Application Trail seemed like a great idea to Bryson... until he did some research, that is. He found that "The woods [are] full of peril—rattlesnakes and water moccasins and nests of copperheads; bobcats, bears, coyotes, wolves, and wild boar; loony hillbillies destabilized by gross quantities of impure corn liquor and generations of profoundly unbiblical sex; rabies-crazed skunks, raccoons, and squirrels; merciless fire ants and ravening blackfly; poison ivy; poison sumac, poison oak, and poison salamanders; even a scattering of moose lethally deranged by a parasitic worm that burrows a nest in their brains and befuddles them into chasing hapless hikers through remote, sunny meadows and into glacial lakes."

I also remembered that most of these nightmarish creatures can be found in the hottest, southern-most states such as North Carolina—great. On top of that, Bryson failed to mention a pair of venomous spiders; the Black Widow and the Brown Recluse. The Black Widow's bite is mild; sometimes you are not aware you have been bitten, but the venom attacks the nervous system causing elevated blood pressure, nausea, sweating and tremors. The Brown Recluse's bite can form a necrotizing ulcer that destroys soft tissue and may take months to heal, leaving deep scars. Just writing about this stuff is giving me the heebie jeebies.

But rest assured! I have been in the U.S. for a good while now and the only thing I have ever seen from this long list was one copperhead snake that was hiding under a patio table. It was a baby and we killed it with a spade.

YOU'RE A RARE AND EXOTIC VOCALIST

As a basketball player you will be treated like a minor celebrity on campus. But if that weren't enough, you also have the English accent going for you. You will receive a steady flow of compliments after you speak and you might start to believe you are a rare and exotic vocalist. But during face-to-face conversations with Americans, be prepared for a lot of seemingly unprovoked smiles, giggles and your fair share of blank stares. There will be times when you won't be sure if anyone is actually listening to what you are saying or just nodding and smiling at the funny way you pronounce your words. You may have seen the movie *Love Actually* where Colin, played by Kris Marshall, is fed up with his lackluster romantic life in the U.K., and travels to the U.S. where he believes he will "get a girlfriend instantly." Shortly after Colin jets across the Atlantic and arrives in Wisconsin, he meets a trio of very attractive women who make him repeat words like "table" and "straw" for their own amusement. Colin obliges by repeating various words while the girls giggle at his pronunciations. But they love it! And Colin is invited back to their house to stay. The belief that American girls love English guys—and their English accents—is not just an old wives' tale. Although this is a movie and all seems slightly exaggerated, it's actually pretty close to reality.

Life in the Colonies

Pronunciation

People in the U.K. are aware of some of the more common differences in pronunciation between American English and what I like to call "the Queen's English". First there are phonetics, the way words are pronounced. In the U.S., you'll hear the American *toMAYto* vs. the English *toMAHto*. You'll hear *aLOOminum* vs. *aluMINium*. Once you make it across the pond you will start ordering *wadder* (not water) to drink in restaurants. On top of that you will have to cope with the differences in vocabulary.

Vocabulary

Americans say "trash can" instead of "bin," "trunk" instead of "boot," and "truck" instead of "lorry." The Queen's English is guaranteed to betray you at some point and you won't even realize it until the blank stares tell you that you've lost your audience. Not long after I arrived in the U.S., my teammates and I visited a sandwich shop (not unlike Subway back in the U.K.) where you choose your bread (white or brown), your meats (turkey, ham, etc.) and then hand select your garnishes (lettuce, onions, etc.) and condiments (mayonnaise, mustard, etc.). When I came towards the last part of the simple process, I asked for lettuce (understood), onions (understood), cucumbers (understood) and lastly, gherkins (blank stare). My sandwich maker had no idea what I was talking about and I couldn't think of an alternative word for "gherkin" so I looked back towards my teammates for help (more blank stares). I started to panic and couldn't even think of a good way to describe a gherkin. Green? No! Everything behind the glass was green. After a lot of pointing and a short process of elimination, the sandwich maker quickly figured out what I was after, "pickles?" he asked.

145

"Pickles!" I said, "Yes, pickles, please." This was my first language learning experience. I dropped "gherkins" from my U.S. vocabulary and sandwich-ordering became a lot easier from that point onwards. I was adapting to survive — Darwin would be proud.

BIG MAN ON CAMPUS

As a college basketball player, you're automatically dubbed as one of the "cool kids on campus." Just make sure this new-found celebrity doesn't go to your head.

Eleven-time NBA All-Star Charles Barkley once said: "I'm not a role model. Just because I dunk a basketball doesn't mean I should raise your kids." Barkley said this after he allegedly spat at a fan that was harassing him. This quote always makes me laugh because what Barkley says is true. Just because Barkley has been blessed with exceptional physical ability doesn't mean that he goes to church, minds his P's and Q's, or helps little old ladies across the street. There is no direct correlation between athletic ability and high moral standing (if there were, it would probably be negative). It just means he's good at basketball. But Americans take their athletics very seriously and treat their professional athletes like superheroes; kids look up to them and adults want to be them. Hence, people expect them to behave in a certain manner (e.g., not spit at fans). And this goes for college athletes, too. Amateur athletics in the U.S. has become so popular that college players are held to the same standards. No matter which college basketball team you play for, you will be in the spotlight. It may shine brighter on some teams than others, but your actions on and off the court will inevitably have far greater consequences. Just like any great superhero, you must choose between good and evil.

You just need to remember: the players who succeed are those who have fun, act kindly to others, and remember to appreciate the great talents they have been given.

DRIVING ON THE 'RIGHT' (CORRECT) SIDE OF THE ROAD

Once you take a couple of car rides in the United States you'll quickly discover that nearly all the cars have automatic transmissions. In my six years in the States, I have seen only two or three manual cars (which Americans call "straight drive"). As you can imagine, automatic cars are a lot easier to drive; they're more like go-karts than automobiles. So when I decided to get my U.S. driver's license, I thought it would be easy. First, I arranged to practice with a friend. I would use his car and he would accompany me on the drive. At first my friend seemed a little nervous with me behind the wheel, but with one less pedal to worry about, what on earth could go wrong? I imagined driving an automatic would be much like driving the go-karts on the Brighton pier. Only my kart was a little bigger and so were the consequences of crashing. Nevertheless, I turned over the engine for the first time with confidence and pulled off my college campus and onto the main roads.

Here's what I didn't realize: the tricky part of driving wasn't operating the vehicle; rather, it was: 1) reading the road signs and figuring out what they meant; and 2) remembering to stay on the correct (right) side of the road. Both were equally as difficult. First, green lights at U.S. intersections don't necessarily mean you have a clear passage through. Sometimes a green light will signal that it's okay for you to make a left turn, but at the same time, oncoming traffic also has the green light to pass straight in front of you—and this oncoming traffic has right-of-way in this instance. Despite being unfamiliar with the laws of the road, and being a"learning-by-doing" type of guy, I soon developed a tactic to help me tackle road intersections. In my short time in the U.S., I had learnt what the term "blitz" meant in relation to American football. Blitz is used to describe the tactic whereby additional players are sent to rush the quarterback and disrupt his attempt to pass the football to a teammate. Essentially, a blitz is a concentration of force at high speed that causes a breakthrough without regard to flanks (in football) or any other oncoming forces. This (idiotically) was the tactic I chose to use when taking on highway intersections, except the referees' whistle was a green light and the flanks were oncoming cars. When the light flicked from red to green I would just hit the gas and hope I made it out of no man's land before I was t-boned by an oversized, gas guzzling, monster truck.

Staying on the correct side of the road was always hardest when I found myself on an empty street with no other cars in sight. Other cars give you your perspective. If I'm driving happily down the road and I see a car driving on the same side of the road but travelling in the opposite direction, that tells me I better get the hell back on the right side of the road. This happened on several occasions. So, this may sound backwards but I would advise that you practice your driving in the U.S. on busier roads. But then again, why would you take my driving advice? I'm not a driving instructor and this isn't a drivers ed book. In any case: drive carefully!

TIPPING

When eating out, remember: good service doesn't come for free. When dining out in the States remember to tip your servers well. Tipping is not compulsory but it's considered good etiquette in restaurants and bars. As a guideline, it would be acceptable to tip 15 percent for good service and 20 percent if you were particularly well-taken care of. So, if you bought dinner for $20 you would leave $3, making your total bill $23 dollars. A little generosity can go a long way, especially if you plan on becoming a repeat customer.

The Last Chapter: Never, Never, Never Give Up

At the end of the day, this book is just words. Having the chance to play college basketball in the United States isn't going to be achieved by talk. It's not going to be done by wishing or hoping. It's going to be done by investing in yourself. You are on a magical journey but only you can conquer the challenges that await you if you are willing to invest. It's your choice. You can be instructed and encouraged, but your ultimate destiny is in your hands.

Remember when I said that Billy Hungrecker used to drop off the *USA Today* on my kitchen counter every day so I could read the NBA box scores? Well, in a few short years something happened that I wouldn't have expected in my wildest dreams. It was on October 31, 2007, to be exact. Our coaches instructed us to meet at the local soda shop in the town of Davidson, just off the college campus. A 'soda shop' is like a café where you can get bar food, burgers, hot dogs, and milkshakes, etc., a type of family restaurant. We were meeting here to get our picture taken by a photographer for a news article. I only later realized that this picture taken with my teammates would appear on the front cover of the *USA Today* sports section beside an article titled *"Hoops, books coexist: Stately Davidson has aura of Ivy but gets high marks on court while taking on nation's power programs."* One moment I was sitting on a wooden bar stool in my kitchen in a farming village in southeast England, and the next moment I am making headlines in one of America's premier newspapers. It just goes to show, keep working, because you never know what's just around the corner.

The 2007-2008 Davidson College Wildcats, en route to an NCAA tournament berth. That's me—just above the guy in the lower-right corner. You might also recognize #30 Stephen Curry, now an NBA All-Star with the Golden State Warriors.

Never, never, never give up.

—WINSTON CHURCHILL

WHY DAVIDSON?

I get asked this questions a lot. When I meet new people and tell them a little about my background, they always ask me, "Why Davidson?"

"Do you want the long or the short version?" I ask, jokingly. Regardless of their answer to my question, I usually stick to the short version to keep myself from turning into a parrot and going insane. But, just this once, I'll give you all the details. And I will even make room for what every good story deserves—a little embellishment.

So, *why Davidson?*

It all started back in England. I went to a public school for my GCSEs but transferred to a private boarding school for sixth form. While I was in sixth form it came time to start applying to university. I did the normal thing and attended talks on how to choose between universities, course offerings and how to put in my application. Eventually, I ended up with applications into six unis using the UCAS system. However, rather than having a couple of top-choice universities and a few backups, all of my UCAS choices were backups. What I really wanted was to attend university in the U.S. So while I began filling in applications, writing personal statements and the like for English universities, I surfed the Internet to research U.S. colleges. I would sit in my dorm room late into the night and browse college Web sites all over the U.S. When I landed on one that looked appealing, I wrote down the name, adding it to the list of schools that stood out. I would also jot down deadlines for submitting my application and any other notes that I found useful.

My boarding house at sixth form was called Middleton. Middleton A, to be exact. A row of detached boarding houses, stretching a half-mile, smack-bang in the middle of campus, made up the 'avenue.' Each boarding house was split into an A and B section and each section had a housemaster. Houses were separated by sex so girls and boys weren't sleeping under the same roof.

Soon after I had completed my UCAS applications I began to knuckle down and fill out my U.S. college applications. I was really alone in this venture. No other sixth formers (that I knew of) were applying to U.S. colleges. However, I realized that there might be one person on campus who could help. There was this one teacher who had a thick American accent. With an accent like that, I thought, he must have spent most of his days stateside and would know a thing or two about U.S. higher education. His name was Dr. Wines and he was a history teacher and housemaster of Peele B. He wasn't my housemaster and I didn't take any of his classes but I had heard him speak in chapel once and we would exchange small talk around campus.

I saw the opportunity to get some information and tips from Dr. Wines and scheduled a meeting with him during prep time (a time shortly after dinner when students are required to be in-house and complete their homework). The evening Dr. Wines and I were scheduled to meet, I finished my homework early and got permission from my housemaster to leave the boarding house. Leaving Middleton A, I walked out into a dark and rainy autumn night. The light escaping from the boarding houses and a few spotlights illuminating the chapel of the century-old school were the only light sources keeping my surroundings visible. All other students were studying safely inside and my only nighttime companion was the Sargent Major[i] who was patrolling the school grounds. I flipped the hood of my coat up over my head to guard me from the rain. I tightened the straps of my backpack, containing a list of prepared questions, and gave a quick "hello" to the Sargent Major before heading down the avenue.

I can't remember the specifics of my conversation with Dr. Wines but I do remember hearing about Davidson College for the first time—coming from his mouth in that twangy southern accent. I had told Dr. Wines what schools I was thinking of applying to and he insisted that I include Davidson to the list. Dr. Wines attended Davidson for two years (1988-1990) and had fallen in love with the college. My applications were already near completion, so adding Davidson only cost me a little more printer toner and the price of postage. After we talked about Davidson for a while, Dr. Wines helped me with some of the peculiar U.S. vernacular on the admissions documents and gave me suggestions for my personal

---

[i] A senior non-commissioned rank or appointment in many militaries around the world applied to the head of security at Christ's Hospital School

statement and essays. He was very eager to help and gave me an open invitation to his office whenever I needed it.

That night I went back to my boarding house and did some research of my own. I found that Davidson was a school in North Carolina on the east coast of the U.S., and the team had won its conference the previous year (2006-2007), losing to Maryland in the NCAA tournament. It looked like a legitimate basketball program but I didn't love it any more than the universities already on my list. From there, I completed and submitted my application to Davidson's admission office just like the 6,800 other hopeful applicants that year. I followed up my application with an email to the head basketball coach saying that I wanted to play basketball for him. Then, I waited for a response.

But again, *"Why Davidson?"*

Here's what I really want to say when someone asks me this question:

"Ask the universe, ask fate, heck, ask God." Did I choose Davidson or did Davidson choose me? I think it was the latter. I was placed into Davidson by Dr. Wines just like Harry Potter was placed into Gryffindor by the sorting hat. If Dr. Wines hadn't been teaching at my sixth form in England I probably would never have heard of the school—even to this day. Whether you believe in fate, you are on a truly magical journey, so enjoy the ride.

But there is one thing I *do* know: I wouldn't have heard about Davidson if I hadn't gone looking for something. The harder I work the more luck I seem to have.

My freshman year (2007-2008), Davidson basketball had one of its finest seasons in school history. We went 20-0 in the Southern Conference (SoCon), became SoCon tournament champions and earned ourselves a spot to compete in the NCAA tournament. We defeated the Gonzaga Bulldogs, the Georgetown Hoyas, and the Wisconsin Badgers to advance to the Elite Eight. We then experienced a heart-breaking exit from the tournament. Down two points with only seconds left in the game, our point guard, Jason Richards, barely missed a three-pointer that would have put us in the Final Four—a true shot at a national championship. We lost to the eventual champion, the Kansas Jayhawks, 59-57. Following the tournament Davidson earned a number-nine ranking in the ESPN/USA Today poll. We were the 9th best college team in the entire United States!

EMAIL FROM DR. WINES TO COACH MCKILLOP

Sent: Sunday, March 23, 2008 11:05 PM
To: McKillop, Bob
Subject: Congratulations from Christ's Hospital, England

Dear Coach McKillop,

Please forgive an intrusion (and a lengthy one at that) from a stranger living 'across the pond' at what must be a very busy time for you.

However, I just wanted to thank you for the immense pleasure that you and your team have given me with your two NCAA tournament victories which I have been able to watch live here in England via the wonders of the Internet. I have two tenuous connections with you. First of all, I attended Davidson from 1988-90 (before heading off to St. Andrews University in Scotland and an 18 year sojourn in the U.K.). As a fanatical college basketball fan I got to witness your first season at Davidson in what was then a brand new sports complex. I remember the grand opening match in the new arena against UVA and the anticipation of Terry Holland's arrival as athletics director. I am ashamed to admit that I was standing with a group of students who were shouting 'come on over now Terry.' The implication, of course, was what was Davidson doing with a high school coach from Long Island when it could have a former school legend and a master of the Division I game at the helm.

How ignorant we were in underestimating your talents and potential.

Secondly, I taught and occasionally played a pick-up game of basketball against Ben Allison here at Christ's Hospital. I believe Woody Kenney was your main contact with Christ's Hospital and to him (and of course to you) should go the credit for bringing Ben to Davidson.

Nevertheless, tonight I am more pleased than ever that I suggested Davidson as a possibility to Ben when he was trying to find a U.S. college and am more certain than ever that he couldn't be part of a finer basketball program.

In closing may I thank you again for those two thrilling victories. I grew up in Virginia and North Carolina with tales of the glories of the old Southern Conference and of the Davidson teams of the 60s. It was magical to see those glories brought back to life this weekend. Best of luck against Wisconsin in Detroit next weekend. If I can ever be of any assistance to you here in the U.K. please do not hesitate to contact me.

Warmest regards,

Andrew Wines
West Lodge
Christ's Hospital

HOW JOSHUA ALLISON DID IT

My brother Josh is two school years older than I, 6′6″ and a pretty decent basketball player. He decided to try his luck playing basketball in the U.S. at Lowcountry Preparatory School, Low Country Preparatory School is a private high school on Pawleys Island in South Carolina. He went there when he was 17 after completing his GCSEs. Josh, like most English players, went to a private high school that was paid for by a sports/academic scholarship. He was set up with a host family and all he had to pay for was food and extras. Lowcountry Prep was a small school and not known for its basketball prowess. Despite a lack of crowd-drawing games on the schedule, Josh was able to use the AAU circuit and a highlight DVD to garner interest from some college programs. He got looks from a few small liberal-arts schools and some bigger Division II colleges. After making his 'official visits' at several schools however, Josh came away feeling like their teams weren't "winning" teams; nor did they have good team chemistry or a winning mentality. He also thought that the overall standard of education seemed poor. For instance, when he sat down with some of the faculty to discuss a possible academic schedule, he felt he had no freedom of choice. Furthermore, the basketball coaches were hesitant for Josh to take certain classes—something that should have never happened: No matter what school you choose to attend, no scholarship basketball player should be banned or discouraged from taking any of the school's courses. Granted, it is true that some bachelor's degrees are easier to obtain than others, meaning they demand a lighter workload, but there should always be viable and manageable options for all student-athletes.

After a number of visits to colleges, Josh couldn't find a place where he felt he could excel both on and off the court. Instead, he chose to return to England to continue his studies. Josh ended up getting a degree in biology with first class honors at the University of Reading, while playing on and off for the Reading Rockets. Later he earned a doctorate in medicine from Imperial College London. The moral of the story is this: if you think that taking a chance on playing basketball in the U.S. will mess up your academic studies, take a look a Josh's case and rest at ease. In order to succeed at anything you have to take risks.

HOW ANDREW LOVEDALE DID IT

Nigerian native, Andrew Lovedale was born on August 24, 1985 in Benin City, Nigeria. He was the eighth of Delphine and Lovedale Ebietomere's 10 children. After his fathers death in 1999, Andrew's life changed drastically. In 2002, Lovedale visited his brother Izevbuwa, a bus driver in London. While there, he continued to play football with his new-found friends, just like back in Nigeria, but soon discovered the Amaechi Basketball Centre in Manchester and was blown away by the caliber of the facilities. "All I wanted to do was further my studies there, so I could play on those beautiful courts and not the ones back home." He later enrolled in school and began to play for the Manchester Magic, a team based out of the Basketball Centre. His coach, Joe Forber, became Andrew's mentor and father figure; he and his wife, Maggie, even attended Andrew's school meetings. Forber left a deep imprint on Andrew's philosophy of life: "He taught me that you can help shape a destiny if you believe and invest in anyone the right way." It was Forber who introduced Andrew to Bob Mckillop and the Davidson basketball program. Coach McKillop, a trusted friend of Joe's, didn't even see Lovedale play basketball before offering him a Division I scholarship at Davidson. He valued Joe's coaching ability and trusted his assessment of Lovedale's ability and character.

Andrew entered Davidson in the fall of 2005, sparking the most intense transition he had ever experienced. He had not visited the college prior to enrolling, and had never even set foot in the U.S. Everything, from the climate to the culture, was new. "I understood how slim my margin for error was, and knew I had to work many times harder than others worked in school, on the court and in life to succeed."

In January of 2008, Andrew, then a junior, became a starting forward on the Wildcats' basketball team. His debut as a starter marked the beginning of the team's rise to underdog fame; they went on to win 25 straight games, the longest college hoops streak in the country, and stole the hearts of March Madness viewers everywhere with three upset wins. Lovedale earned All-Southern Conference honours after a senior season in which he averaged 12.5 points and 8.6 rebounds (second best in the Southern Conference).

Looking back, Lovedale believes it was not just his skills on the court that landed him a scholarship. "Take your education as seriously as you take your basketball," he says. "By doing so, you understand that the need to maximize both platforms is necessary to live a good life."

TEAM G.B: OFF-DAY IN ROMANIA

Off days can get you in a lot of trouble. If, one day, you play basketball in college or even for a professional team, you will become familiar with the term "off day." Usually college teams practice six days a week. In NCAA basketball, coaches are required to give their players one off day a week, during which they have no compulsory basketball activities. Some see an off day as a time to get some well-needed rest while others see it as a great opportunity to let off some steam. While in Romania in 2008, playing for Great Britain U21's in the European championships, my teammates and I saw it as the latter.

European championships are typically scheduled so teams get one off day during the tournament. There are no games that day but the teams may practice. At dinner the night before our off day, our head coach stands up and makes an announcement. He reminds us that we have an off day the next day but we have a 10 p.m. curfew that night.

Now, in my teammates' and my defense, before I tell the rest of the story, elite basketball players don't tend to be the most introverted people in the world. More often than not, the best athletes tend to be confident (even arrogant), more sociable than the average person, and highly susceptible to taking risks. Also, you have to bear in mind that we had been coupled up in a tiny European hotel in Transylvania, Romania. That's right, Dracula's old stomping ground. In fact, I hope he's still there, for the story goes that a small group of men and women, led by Professor Van Helsing is the only thing stopping Dracula's attempt to move from Transylvania to England. If you're not familiar with the tales of Count Dracula, think turreted castles high up in the mountains; vampires and stray rabies-infested dogs roaming the streets. I'm not sure why this was chosen as the location for the 2008 European

Championships; the closest airport was over 3 hours' drive from the hotel and our team bus barely made it up the winding mountain roads. Anyway, we had been cooped up in our hotel rooms for days eating Milka chocolate bars and watching CNN (the only English-speaking TV channel). We needed a night out.

After dinner, I talked with some of my teammates. We were thinking of breaking curfew and hitting a couple of bars and clubs in the area. That year, I was team co-captain and took the lead on organizing our little outing. I decided to make it a team activity and pretty much made it mandatory for everyone to participate (see how I'm taking the hit for this one). The word spread through the team that we were all going to make sure we were in our hotel rooms at 10 p.m. We then ordered three or four taxis to arrive at the back of the hotel—this was so we didn't have to walk through the main lobby and past the hotel bar/restaurant where our coaches were possibly hanging out. Our naive selves thought this was a pretty foolproof plan. For awhile everything was going well. We forfeited the elevators and chose the back stairs as a more discreet exit and jumped into the taxis waiting outside. We asked the drivers to take us to the best club in Transylvania (which turned out to be also the worst club in Transylvania because it was the *only* club in the godforsaken city). But when we arrived we found the place hopping. It was a large club with multiple dance floors, go-go dancers[ii], and a plethora of cute women.

[ii] **Go-go dancers** are dancers employed to entertain crowds at a discotheque. Their classic image is a short dress and tall boots.

We went straight over to the bar and started ordering flaming Lamborghini's to drink. A flaming Lamborghini is made from liqueurs Kahlua, Sambuca, Blue Curacao and Bailey's Irish Cream… and then set on fire! You pour the Sambuca and Kahlua into a cocktail glass, pour the Bailey's and Blue Curacao into two separate shot glasses (either side of the cocktail glass), light the concoction in the cocktail glass and drink it (all in one) through a straw. As you reach the bottom of the glass, you put out the fire by pouring the Bailey's and Blue Curacao into the cocktail glass and keep drinking till it's gone.[1] Holy smokes, we were living large, blowing off steam, relaxing, making new friends and partying the night away…

Then the shit hit the fan.

I'm sitting down on a small couch just off the dance floor, drink in hand, and I see this girl striding directly toward me from the middle of the dance floor. I didn't recognize her and wondered what she was going to say. In her non-British accent she said "I think dat your coaches ah ear," and then pointed behind her toward the entrance. Slightly panicked, I set down my drink and used the armrest to lift myself just high enough so I could see the entrance over the crowd of people.

"Shit!"

The entire GB coaching staff was standing just inside the club surveying the people within. The next part is kind of funny. Owing to the fact that the people that make up a basketball team are typically at least a foot taller than the general population, even in a crowded public space, I can usually see all of my teammates all the time—or at least their heads and shoulders. I stood up and tried to make eye contact. As soon as I make eye contact with one of my teammates and alerted him to our situation the message was relayed across the club like the fire beacons used in the 16-century to relay messages along the coastline of approaching raiders. As soon as one person realized what was up he made eye contact with the next. And at this moment we were probably as scared of our coaches as the English were of the Spanish Armada. The message was relayed very quickly and the next logical step was to duck and cover. In an instant all of the tall people who were in the club a moment before had suddenly disappeared. One of my teammates was so extreme in his attempt to stay of our sign that he was actually crawling on the floor of the club in a slew of trodden in filth and spilled alcohol.

The entire team managed to make their way to a small bathroom on the ground floor where we congregated.

"Was anyone seen" one of my teammates asked. Everyone began to speak all at once; it was like a community board meeting at the town hall. We came to the conclusion that, chances are, pretty much everyone has been seen. We decided to walk back out and reveal ourselves to the coaches. We would stay at the club for a while longer before making our way back to the hotel, and accept our punishment the next day.

Here's what we didn't know: the next day the performance director for Great Britain Basketball was flying into Romania to meet with the team and coaches and watch practice. Instead of watching a typical GB practice of talented basketball players, he watched us run laps around the court for an entire two hours. I'm not exaggerating. We didn't touch a basketball that day. As punishment for our crime, we ran, we ran, and we ran some more.

We were all so relieved when coach told us practice was over. We were all ready to take off our shoes, nurse our burning feet and get back to the hotel we were so eager to leave the night before. Instead, however, our coach dismissed the empty busses and made us run the four-mile trip back. This was the cherry on the cake. But looking back, we deserved every bit of our punishment.

GLOSSARY OF TERMS

Amateur
One who has never accepted money, or who accepts money under restrictions specified by a regulatory body for participating in a competition (According to the NCAA)

AND1
An American athletic shoe company specializing in basketball shoes and clothing

Athletic Scholarship
A form of financial aid to attend a college or university, or a private high school, awarded to an individual based predominantly on ability to play a sport

Big Dance
Another name for the NCAA Men's Division I Basketball Championship, a single-elimination tournament held each spring in the United States, featuring 68 college basketball teams

BBL
The premier men's professional basketball league in the United Kingdom

Class rank
Measure of how a student's performance compares to other students in a graduating class; Often expressed as a percentile; e.g., a student in a class of 800, who has a higher GPA than 750 classmates, is in the top 10 percent of the class.

College
Generic term in American English that refers to: A) the next level of education after high

school; B) a place of higher learning (see University); C) a constituent part of a university. Americans often use "college" and "university" interchangeably.

College Board U.S. organization that issues and regulates the Scholastic Assessment Test (SAT)

Common Application (Informally, the "Common App") An undergraduate college admission application used to apply to any of 415 member colleges and universities in the United States

Compliance Officer Officer primarily responsible for overseeing and managing regulatory NCAA compliance issues for a particular college

Cover Letter A clarifying document that is usually sent along with an application of some sort

Customs (Formally Customs and Border Protection) A U.S. government department, part of the Department of Homeland Security, responsible for securing the international border and enforcing immigration laws

DSO (Designated School Official) Employee of a U.S. college responsible for creating I-20s, SEVIS records, and representing the school in all matters related to F-1 and M-1 students

Division I The highest level of U.S. intercollegiate athletics sanctioned by the NCAA

Division II   Less commercial level than NCAA Division I but still offers athletic scholarships to student-athletes

Division III   The NCAA's non-commercial level of U.S. intercollegiate athletics; D-III schools offer academic scholarships but not athletic scholarships

DS-160   Online Non-immigrant Visa Application form used for temporary travel to the United States.

Eligibility   Student-athlete's status (as determined by the NCAA) that allows him or her to compete in intercollegiate athletics. Once student-athletes (and prospective student-athletes) are cleared to compete, they must continue to meet academic and amateurism benchmarks to stay eligible.

Equivalency Sport   NCAA sport that can offer full or partial scholarships; Sports other than: men's basketball, women's basketball, (American) football, women's gymnastics, women's tennis, women's volleyball

F-1 Student Visa   The most common type of visa for those who wish to engage in academic studies in the United States.

Federal Taxes   Taxes that must be paid to the U.S. government; Foreign individuals and corporations not residing in the U.S. must pay this tax on income from a U.S. business and certain types of income from U.S. sources.

GPA

Grade Point Average; The average of all your academic grades

Head Count Sport

NCAA sport that offers full scholarships only: men's basketball, women's basketball, football, women's gymnastics, women's tennis, and women's volleyball

Highlight DVD

The #1 tool in the recruitment process; Footage can be edited on a computer and burned to a DVD.

Homeland Security

The U.S. government department that administers all matters relating to U.S. border security

Host Family

A family assigned to an international student that will include the student in family activities, enriching his or her stay, providing a true picture of American culture.

I-20

A form issued in your name by the school or schools to which you have applied and been accepted. These schools must be SEVP-certified schools.

I-94

Form denoting the Arrival-Departure record of particular foreigners used by U.S. Customs and Border Protection

iMovie   Apple's proprietary video editing software application; typically comes preinstalled on Apple computers.

Inter Eligibility Center   (Also known as the NCAA Initial- Eligibility Clearinghouse) Organization that works with the NCAA to determine a student's eligibility for athletics participation in the first year of college enrollment; Students who want to participate in college sports during their first year of college enrollment must register with the clearinghouse.

International Advisor   See DSO.

Junior College   A college offering courses for two years beyond high school, either as a complete training or preparation for completion at a four-year college.

Liberal Arts School   School with a primary emphasis on undergraduate study in the liberal arts and sciences.

Major conference   One of any six conferences considered the most competitive in NCAA competition: the ACC, SEC, Big East, Big 10, Big 12 and Pac-12

March Madness   Time of the annual NCAA college basketball tournament, generally throughout the month of March

Glossary

Mid-Major Term used to refer to athletic conferences that are not among the six majors but are still highly competitive

Movie Maker Microsoft's freeware video editing software; Part of Windows Essentials software suite and offers the ability to create and edit videos

NAIA The National Association of Intercollegiate Athletics: a governing body that oversees college and university-level athletic programs at four-year, non-NCAA member schools

NBA National Basketball Association: the pre-eminent men's professional basketball league in North America, arguably the world

NCAA The National Collegiate Athletic Association: a nonprofit association of 1,281 institutions, conferences, organizations and individuals that govern the athletic programs of many colleges and universities in the U.S. and Canada.

NIT National Invitational Tournament: a men's college basketball tournament operated by the NCAA

NJCAA The National Junior College Athletic Association: a governing body of athletic programs at community and junior colleges throughout the U.S.

Official Visit An athletics recruiting visit to a U.S. college financed in whole or in part by the institution

Partial Scholarship A scholarship that covers part of the tuition and boarding costs

Postgraduate year Extra year of U.S. high school before enrolling in college; often spent at an independent (private) school

Prep School U.S. high school whose mission is to prepare students for college; Often (but not always) a private (not government-supported) school

Private School North American school supported primarily by private (non-government) funds

Public School North American school supported primarily by public (government) funds.

Redshirt A college athlete who does not participate in intercollegiate competition for one year, in order to develop skills and extend by one year the period of playing eligibility

Reference Written statement from a person who can vouch for your qualities and strengths

Retake (Usually with respect to an examination) Sitting an exam for a second (or additional) time

Response Set Tendency for a test-taker to answer a series of questions a certain way and on a consistent

Glossary

basis; e.g., a response set called acquiescence refers to the tendency to respond "true" or "yes" to questionnaire items, regardless of the prompts

SAT Testing Center A location, usually at a school or university, where you can sit the SAT

SEVIS Receipt Proof of payment of the SEVIS I-901 fee, the electronic record in SEVIS, and the I-901 payment system; in most cases, people who need to verify payment can do so electronically.

SAT Standardized Aptitude Test: a U.S. standardized test for most college admissions

State School See: Public School; May also refer to public institutions of post-secondary education.

State Taxes Taxes on earnings you may have to pay, depending on that U.S. state's imposition of tax

Streetball An informal type of basketball played, usually in such urban areas as parking lots and playgrounds

Student-Athlete Participant in an organized competitive sport sponsored by the educational institution where the student is enrolled; Often used to describe the life balance of a full-time student and a full-time athlete

Glossary

Student Union A building on a college campus dedicated to social and organizational activities of the student body

Study Hall The period of time in a school curriculum set aside for study and the preparation of schoolwork

University Educational institution designed for instruction and examination of students in many branches of advanced learning, conferring degrees in various faculties, and often embodying colleges and similar institutions

Visa Application Fee The fee due to the U.S. Department of Homeland Security for processing your visa.

Year in residence One (academic) year when a student-athlete lives at the school and practices with the team but does not play in contests; This often affects Division I student-athletes who transfer from a two-year school and do not meet transfer requirements, or transfer from one four-year school to another four-year school.

ACKNOWLEDGMENTS

First, I must thank Coach **Bob McKillop,** without whom, this book would not have been possible. Time and again, McKillop has shown incredible trust and belief in me. He believes in people when they don't believe in themselves. He dreams fanciful dreams and then turns them into reality. I can't wait to see what's next.

Judge Joe Craig, you have been such a great friend and supporter of all my projects. Your wisdom and flair for writing helped turn this book into something special.

Larry Dagenhart, Jr., your passion for helping people and care for people around you is unparalleled. You have a genuine and infectious love for storytelling that has helped carry me through the ebbs in writing. I can't thank you enough.

Coach Woody Kenny, living the life out in California. You have such a positive outlook on life that has inspired me throughout my basketball career. Thanks for the good times!

Works Cited

Chapter 1

[1] Kansas, Dave. "Why Do the British Stink at Basketball?" *The Wall Street Journal.* 19 August 2010. Web. 20 May. 2013

Chapter 2

[1] O'Toole, Thomas. "NCAA reached 14-year deal with CBS/Turner for men's basketball tournament, which expands to 68 teams for now." *USA Today.* 22 April 2010. Web. 26 May 2013.

[2] MrSEC.com. "NCAA tournament: The Money Behind the Madness." *Mr. SEC.com.* March 21 2013. Web. May 10 2013.

[3] Gibson, Owen. "British Basketball gets Olympic funding reprieve after UK Sport Appeal. *The Guardian.* February 1 2013. Web. Feb 16 2013.

[4] Kansas, Dave. "Why Do the British Stink at Basketball?" *The Wall Street Journal.* 19 August 2010. Web. 20 May. 2013

[5] "Foreign Players In America." *USBasket.* 3 January 2014. Web. 10 May 2013.www.usbasket.com.

[6] Kansas, Dave. "Why Do the British Stink at Basketball?" *The Wall Street Journal.* 19 August 2010. Web. 20 May. 2013.

[7] Zegers, Charlie. "One and Done" *About.com.* Web. www.basketball.about.com

8 Dauston, Rob. "Will new academic standards impact college hoops' on-court product?" *NBC Sports.* 24 September 2012. Web 8 July 2013.

Chapter 3

1 Murdock, Marie. "The Average College Tuition Costs in the United States". *eHow.* 5 July 2013. Web. 26 May 2013.

2 "What is the difference between NCAA Division I, II, III and NAIA?" *Hoops Plus, LLC.* Web. 5 October 2013. www.hoopsplus.org

3 "What is the difference between NCAA Division I, II, III and NAIA?" *Hoops Plus, LLC.* Web. 5 October 2013. www.hoopsplus.org

4 "What is the difference between NCAA Division I, II, III and NAIA?" *Hoops Plus, LLC.* Web. 5 October 2013. www.hoopsplus.org

5 "What is an Athletic Scholarship?" *College Sports Scholarships.* Web. www.collegesportsscholarships.com

6 "College Basketball Scholarships and Recruiting" *Athnet.* Web. www.athleticscholarships.net

7 "2013-2014 Division I School Affiliations" *RPI Ratings.* Web. 7 May 2013. www.rpiratings.com.

8 "Foreign Student (F-1) in Public Schools." *Travel.State.Gov.* Web. www.travel.state.gov/visa.

[9] Cann, Warwick. " British Basketball players studying and playing in the US." PDF file. www.gbbasketball.com

[10] Web. Aug. 17 2013. www.ask.com.

[11] Web. March 10 2013. www.voanews.com.

Chapter 4

[1] Rampell, Catherine. "The Recession Has (Officially) Ended". *The New York Times.* 20 September 2010. Web. 14 November 2013.

[2] Gibbs, Megan. "The Athlete's Official Visit" *College Xpress.* 27 Nov. 2012. Web. 22 September 2013.

[3] Adrian Wojnarowski. "The Miracle of St. Anthony."p 68-69.

Chapter 5

[1] YouTube. 6 Oct. 2013. Web. [Video File]. www.youtube.com

[2] Schweitzer, Karen. "SAT Tips for Test Day" *About.com.* Web.

[3] "Average College Acceptance Rates Can Inspire Or Paralyze. Here's What You Can Do About It" 12 April 2013. Web. www.oncampusdialogue.com.

[4] Burrell, Jackie. "The High Cost of College Applications" *About.com.* Web. 3 June 2013.

Chapter 6

[1] "Department of Homeland Security" *U.S. Department of Homeland Security.* Web. 22 August 2013. www.ice.gov

Chapter 7

[1] King, Jason. "Juco Transfer in the Spotlight." *ESPN Men's Baksetball.* 1 Nov. 2011. Web. 3 March 2013.

[2] Cann, Warwick. " British Basketball players studying and playing in the US." PDF file. www.gbbasketball.com

[3] Cann, Warwick. " British Basketball players studying and playing in the US." PDF file. www.gbbasketball.com

[4] Taylor, Jim. "The Power of Prime." *Psychology Today.* 30 March 2011. Web. 14 May 2013.

Chapter 8

[1] Fong, Bethany. "Balanced Diet for a Basketball Player." *Livestrong.com.* 27 August 2013. Web. 6 May 2013.

[2] "Michael Phelps' 12,000 Calorie-a-Day Diet Not for Everyone." *Fox News.* 14 August 2008. Web. 6 May 2013.

[3] Web. 1 Oct 2013. Studyusa.com

Chapter 9

[1] Web. 1 Dec 2013. www.drinksmixer.com

Printed in Great Britain
by Amazon